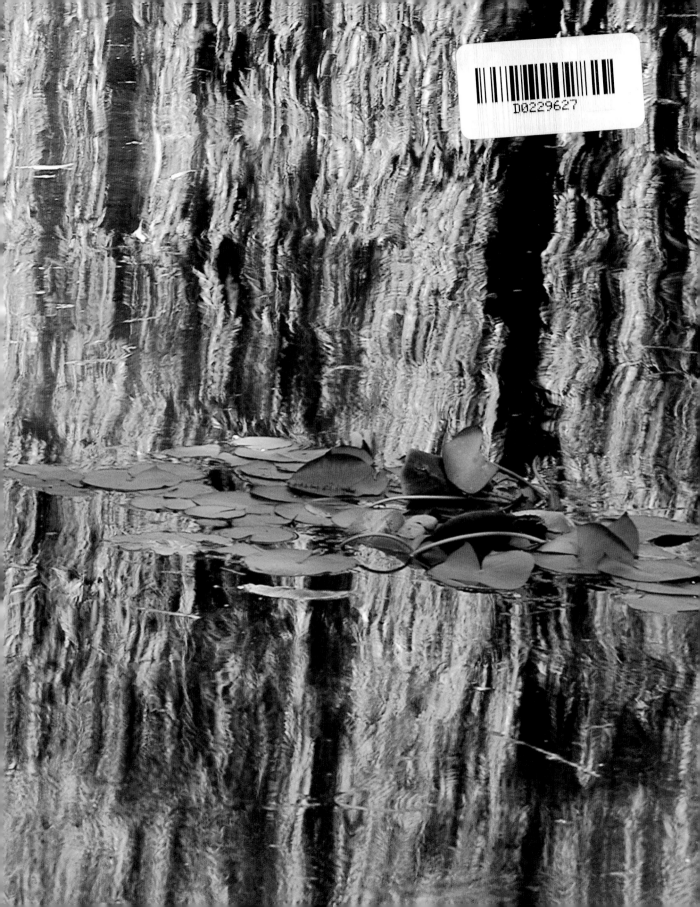

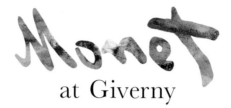

Monet
at Giverny

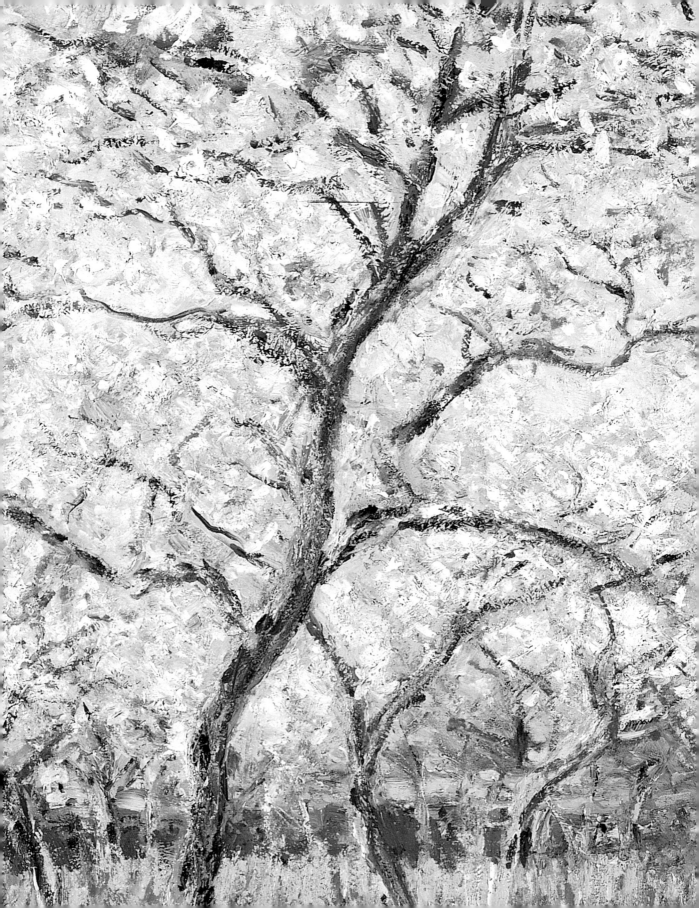

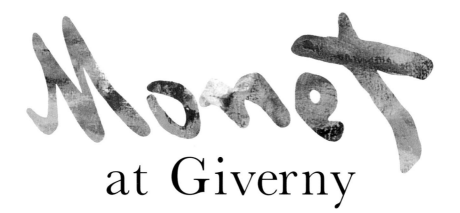

Monet
at Giverny

CAROLINE HOLMES

CASSELL&co

To my parents whose love of family, zest
for life, sense of humour and love of France
are the greatest gifts I have had and can
hope to give.

First published in the United Kingdom in 2001
by Cassell & Co

Distributed in the United States of America by
Sterling Publishing Co., Inc.
387 Park Avenue South
New York
NY 10016 - 8810

The photographic acknowledgements on page 192 constitute
an extension to this copyright page.

A CIP catalogue record for this book is available from
the British Library.

ISBN 0304 359009

Editor Catherine Bradley
Design Director David Rowley
Designer Clive Hayball
Indexer Kathy Gill

Typeset in Baskerville M T
Bauer Bodoni BT and Helvetica Neue
Printed and bound in Italy by Printer Trento S.r.l.

Endpapers: © Vivian Russell

Cassell & Co Wellington House
125 Strand London WC2R 0BB

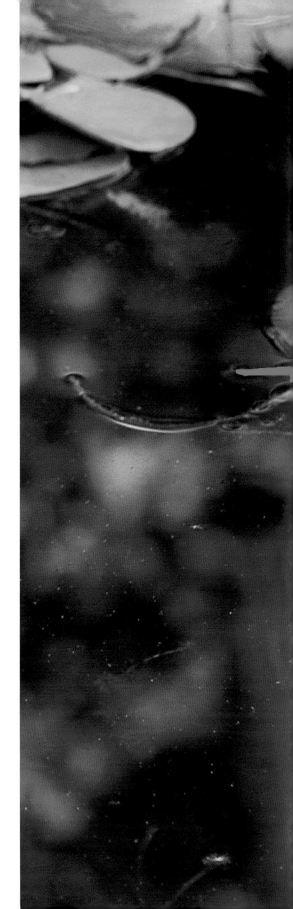

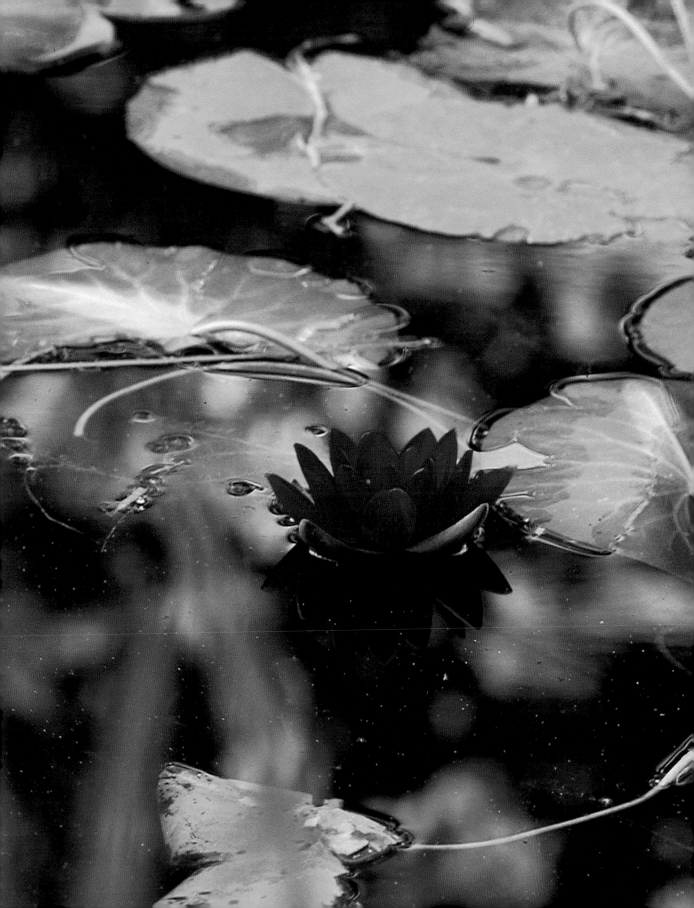

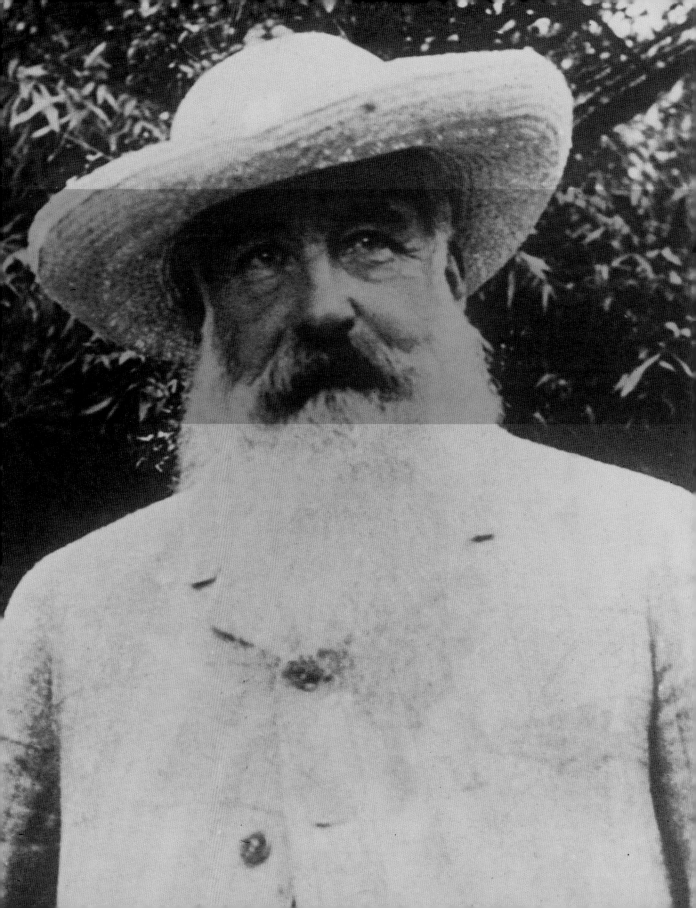

Contents

Introduction

The road bringing me to Monet and his 43 years of life and work at Giverny has been long and sometimes surprising. Even when my taste for certain of his paintings has stayed the same, I have found that over the course of time my perception of them – of why they should move me – has undergone a radical change. This change of response to his work was an experience with which Monet himself was familiar.

Monet and his works have been present in my life since my earliest years – one might say from before that time. In 1927, the year after his death, the Musée de l'Orangerie opened its doors on his monument to the dead of World War I, in which his serene *Grandes Décorations* project depicted the gardens at Giverny. It was in the same year that my grandfather, having spent six months in Hollywood, arrived in Paris with his wife and small son to work as an adviser on converting silent screen cinemas to show the new sound films. From 1927 to 1937, the family rented a house on the outskirts of the city, in Rue Corot, Ville d'Avray, where the elderly owner had known both Corot and Monet as neighbours and near where, in 1866, Monet had painted *Women in the Garden*. Listening to family reminiscences of the place as a small child in 1960, at the same time I entertained myself by looking at the pictures in a large book by William Seitz, simply entitled *Monet*, which my father had bought whilst working in Italy. Forty years later I had come to know Seitz's book as a major turning-point in the reassessment of Monet's work. In 1989 my five year old son Nick and I went to the 'Monet in the Nineties' exhibition at the Royal Academy of Arts in London, our two pairs of eyes observing the works, one with childish openness, the other informed by my taste in gardens. Regrettably, the gardener wondered ignorantly how anyone could have the tenacity to paint the same motif so many times.

The child chatted confidently about all the different colours and lights you could see, and how much more enjoyable they were when the subject stayed the same. Eleven years later, returning for 'Monet in the 20th Century', if not better informed we were without a doubt differently programmed.

In the same way Monet, having viewed Turner's paintings in 1870 during several months spent in London, claimed to be unimpressed; however, on his return twenty years later he revised his opinion. Was it the artist or the gardener that had wrought this change? Certainly the two can be famously intermingled. Gertrude Jekyll, often described as England's 'Impressionist gardener', claimed that Turner's *Fighting Temeraire* had been the inspiration for the colour schemes, designed in the early decades of the 20th century, that elegantly drifted through many of her great herbaceous borders.

After Gerald Van der Kemp's major restorations at Giverny from 1977, I read avidly about the reincarnation of Monet's garden. In 1990 my chance came to know the place as intimately as I wished. Since I spoke French, and knew the Loire valley well, I was offered the chance to devise and host a tour of French gardens. Where better to start, before heading south to the Loire, than Monet's garden at Giverny?

In July 1991 the upper garden, with its arbours, walks and flowerbeds, looked dry and a little tired. But following the paths that led enticingly to the verdant serenity of the water garden, I found I was hooked; thereafter I visited at least once, and often three times, every year. From its deep winter appearance, rather like that of a sodden cat, in spring the upper garden fluffs up into a state of exuberance, its impressionistic haze of colour contrasting with the water garden's other world of calm, elegant simplicity. An absurd number of visitors can be absorbed by the water garden – and still it can exude tranquillity. The resulting income has paid for a useful irrigation system, but some token form of barrier now has to hold back the many eager feet following Monet's ghost to the water's edge or across the upper lawns.

Alone, with family or hosting groups for a variety of public and private organizations, I have made regular trips between Giverny and three key museums in Paris – the Musées d'Orsay, Marmottan and de l'Orangerie (the last still closed at the time of writing). At the Musée d'Orsay, a former railway station affectionately known as MD'O, I enjoy the architecture, with its splendid contrast between the heavy 19th-century style of the first class waiting rooms and the light roomy platforms. The museum's collections of French art post 1848 enable the visitor to compare and contrast Monet with his contemporaries. The Marmottan, whilst offering a prodigious chronology of Monet's work austerely displayed, also illustrates the way in which the *haut-bourgeois* Marmottan family lived and acquired their art, in contrast to Monet's more personal and eclectic collection. The two oval basements of the Orangerie are devoted to Monet's great patriotic testament to the serenity of his garden as represented by his water lilies. The joy of these four places is visually and intellectually accessible, but their pleasures are also of the kind that increase with acquaintance – just as gardeners learn to cherish the maturing of their own skills through knowledge and experience.

In the years that Monet lived at Giverny, the house and garden became his life blood, transfusing their natural rhythms and harmonies into his spirit and intellect. To continue the metaphor, Blanche Hoschedé, both step-daughter and daughter-in-law to Monet, kept the property on a life-support system until her death 20 years later. This *bois dormant*, this Sleeping Beauty, was thereby lost not only among the equivalent of fairytale brambles; her beds and frames had disappeared too, and the sinuous banks of the water garden had been seriously eroded. To reawaken Giverny would need a considerable transfusion of money and talent. In 1976 Gerald Van der Kemp appointed the young Gilbert Vahé, now head gardener, from the École Nationale d'Horticole at Versailles to restore the landscaping of Giverny, together with an administrator, now Director, Claudette Lindsey. Our knowledge and understanding of Giverny is deeply indebted to their experience and the success of their efforts.

When Monet started painting at Giverny, he reckoned changes of light in half-hour intervals. But, by the end of his life, habits of close observation had ensured that his perception of light changes was sophisticated enough to judge them by intervals of just a few minutes. Today's visitor of two or three hours duration does well to remember this when trying to identify with a fraction of those 43 years of concentrated work.

Before entering the gardens, head west up the village street to the faded Hotel Baudy; I have an abiding memory of a soup plate-sized peony being lovingly shaded by its own large white parasol in the gardens of the hotel. This is where in Monet's time several young American artists stayed; their garden *atelier* is still there to be seen today. As you leave, look north to the nearby hills and south past plane trees and poplars to the River Seine. Savour the seasonal atmosphere as you stroll back and, well prepared, enter Monet's domain, by way of the house. Remember to explore the kitchen (one way to Monet's heart was always through his stomach), and in your mind's ear convert the chatter of other tourists into guests gathered in his living room.

Like most in Giverny, Monet's house lies on an east-west axis, so that bright light, playing across poplars, willows and cherries, can come in through the windows – including those of his former bedroom – from sunrise to sunset. The veranda, built by Monet, skilfully links house and garden. From it one can survey the central axis, down the Grande Allée and on to the copper beech planted as a climax to this vista. As late summer approaches, you will appreciate that this path is more than a formal walk. The sky and the gravel become hidden outside a verdant tunnel, with roof woven by roses and walls a tapestry of flowers; below lie footings of vigorous trailing nasturtiums. Outside the Grande Allée, relish the clematis 'rooms' and the grid of flowerbeds in a deliberate choice of paintbox colours.

A road separates the two gardens, and crossing this today would shatter any coherent enjoyment; however, with the restoration has come a tunnel to the water garden. Here light seems forever to change, the atmosphere greened by willows and bamboos as the path curves along the pool's edge to the Japanese Bridge swathed in wisterias. Despite the innumerable reproductions of paintings showing this scene the physical reality still astonishes, with the water lilies bright in their liquid medium. In your imagination, play with the horizon and with the pool's reflections, the mirror images of the rose arbour and the bridges, and ask where the sky begins and the water ends.

Giverny and Monet are inseparable. The inspiration of the artist served to shape an individual, evolving domain, which in turn informed many of his great paintings. The interplay of light and colour, foliage and canvas was distilled at Giverny into a powerful creative impetus. It provided an intense, sensual environment to which Monet's artistic vision would continually respond.

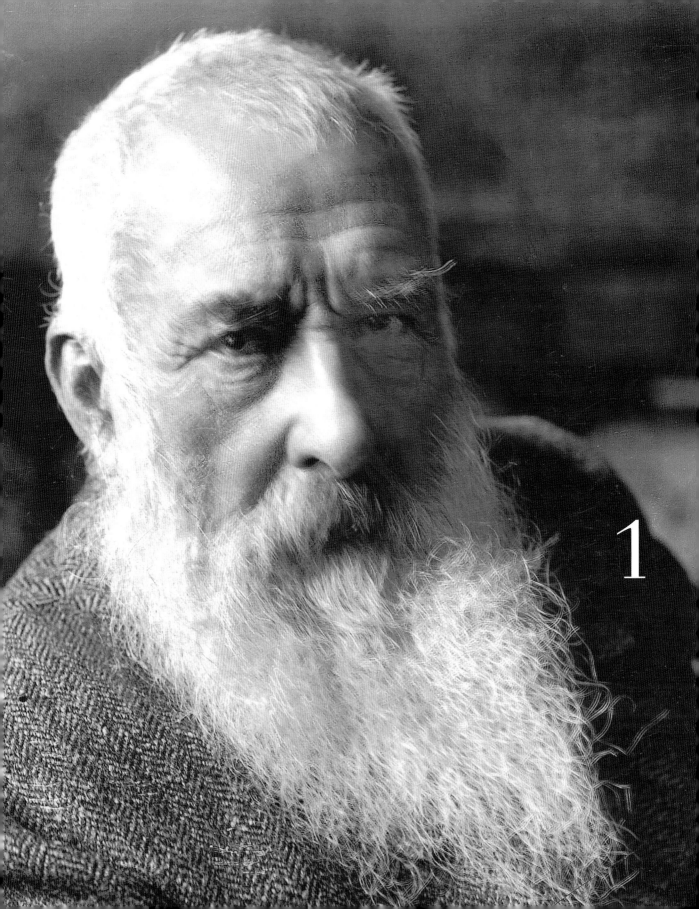

The Man

The mind of an artist

DURING HIS YEARS at Giverny, Monet's daily routine seldom varied. He woke early, at four or five. Opening the window, he would study the sky. If the dawn augured well for that day's weather he would take a cold bath, followed at 5.30 am by a hearty breakfast. He then set off to paint, sometimes with members of his family as helpers, returning at 11.00 am. Lunch had to be served on the dot of 11.30 am, and was followed by coffee and home-made plum brandy. After a short rest he resumed work out of doors, observing changes in the sky as reflected in the nearby river or, in later years, by the pool in his garden; alternatively he would paint in his studio. The bell for dinner would ring at 7.00 pm, and bedtime, like Monet's hour of rising, was early, at 9.30 pm. Any variation in this daily routine was extremely unwelcome, and he would be most displeased if he had had a bad day or the sky had not been to his liking. However, this rigid timetable was no obstacle to the generous hospitality shown over the years towards many friends and relatives, for whom Giverny became the heart of a large extended family.

In the six years before the Monets' arrival at Giverny, personal extravagance and a lack of commissions had impoverished both them and their friends and

Below Photography held little interest for Monet as part of the artistic process, unlike contemporaries such as Delacroix. However, it was a popular family pastime in the Monet-Hoschedé household. In one of his own rare photographs, the shadow of his brimmed hat nestles below the water lilies.

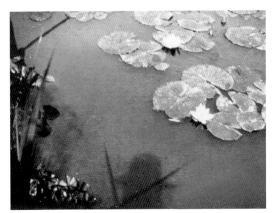

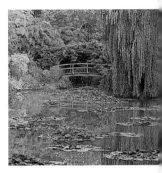

Above By 1903 the pool at Giverny had been lengthened to 60 m (197 ft) and an upper gallery had been added to the bridge. The water lilies produced a tide of colour.

Right Monet defined these almost abstract lily pads with bold loops of paint that seem to float on the canvas. In this atmospheric detail from **Water Lilies: Green Reflections**, *1916–26*, the sky and willows are reflected as textured strands.

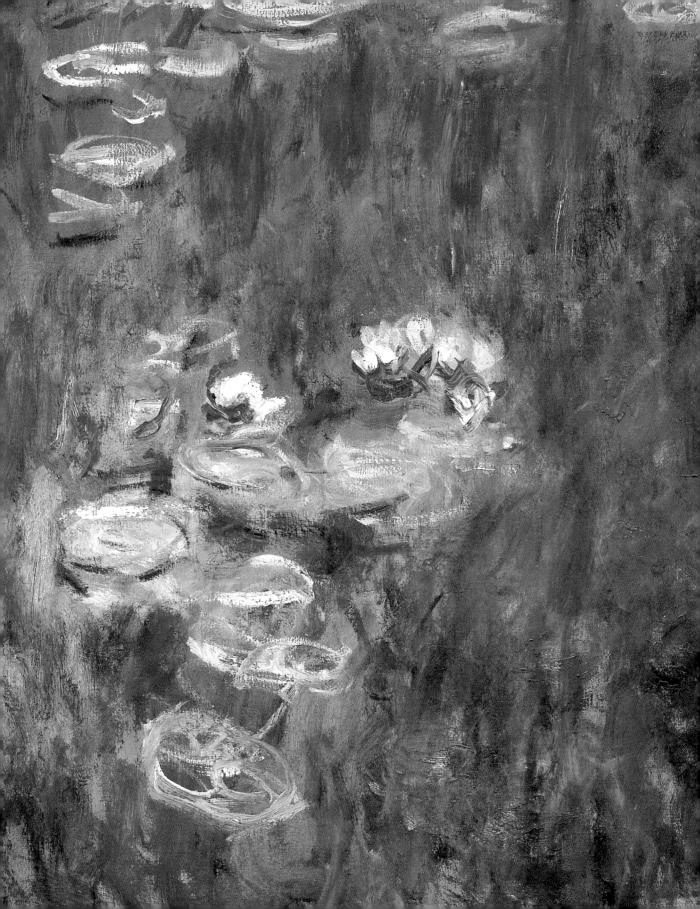

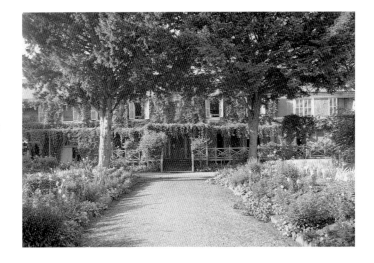

Right Monet added a terrace to his house at Giverny, later covered by a canopy swathed in plants. In summer the pink façade gradually disappeared under a Virginia creeper. A pair of yew trees frame the vista up the Grande Allée to the door.

patrons the Hoschedés. Faced with bankruptcy, their benefactor, the once wealthy industrialist Ernest Hoschedé, deserted his family, leaving his wife, Alice, pregnant with their sixth child, Jean-Pierre. When in 1878 the Monets moved out of Paris to Vétheuil, a few kilometres down the Seine, they were joined by Alice Hoschedé and her children. Shortly before, in March of that year, Camille Monet gave birth to a son, Michel. A painful long-term womb infection followed, and in September 1879 Camille died. The Monet and Hoschedé families continued to live as one household, notwithstanding several changes of address; between 1881 and 1883 they moved the short distance from Vétheuil to Poissy, then they decamped to Pourville on the coast near Dieppe for a few summer months, thence back to Poissy.

In 1883, Monet was halfway through his life, the canvas of the man marked by emotional and professional contrasts of

Right Vibrant colours of flowers dominate the Grande Allée in Monet's vision of **The Garden, Giverny**, *1902*. The intense hues of flowers gleam in the sun on the facing carp's back beds.

'Don't you find that one does better when all

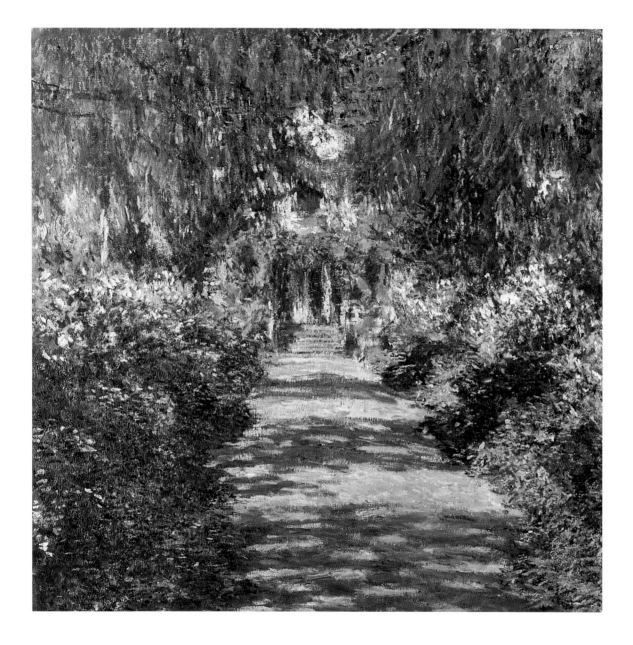

alone with nature? I myself am convinced of it.'

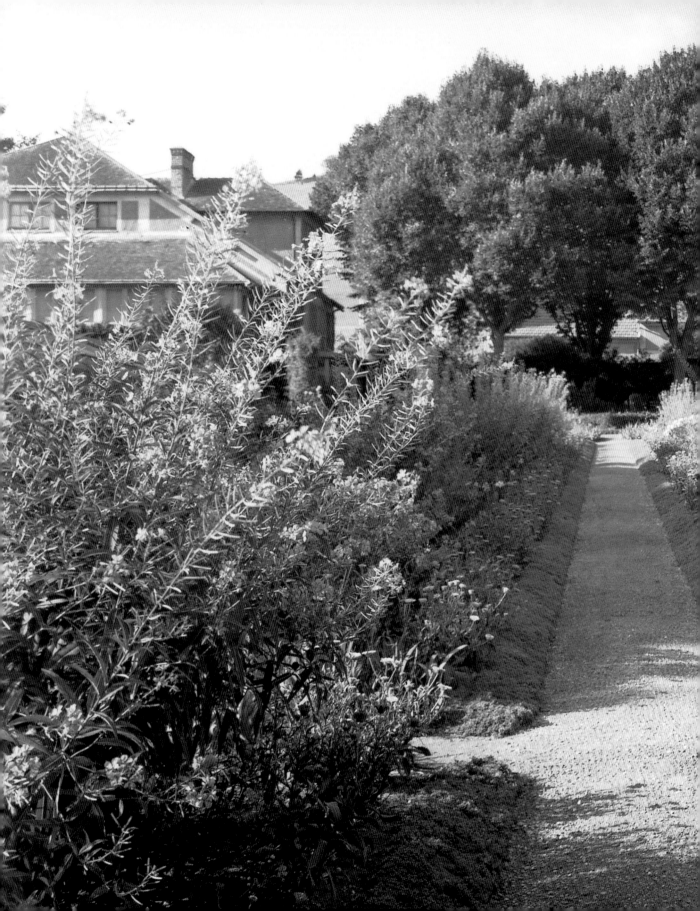

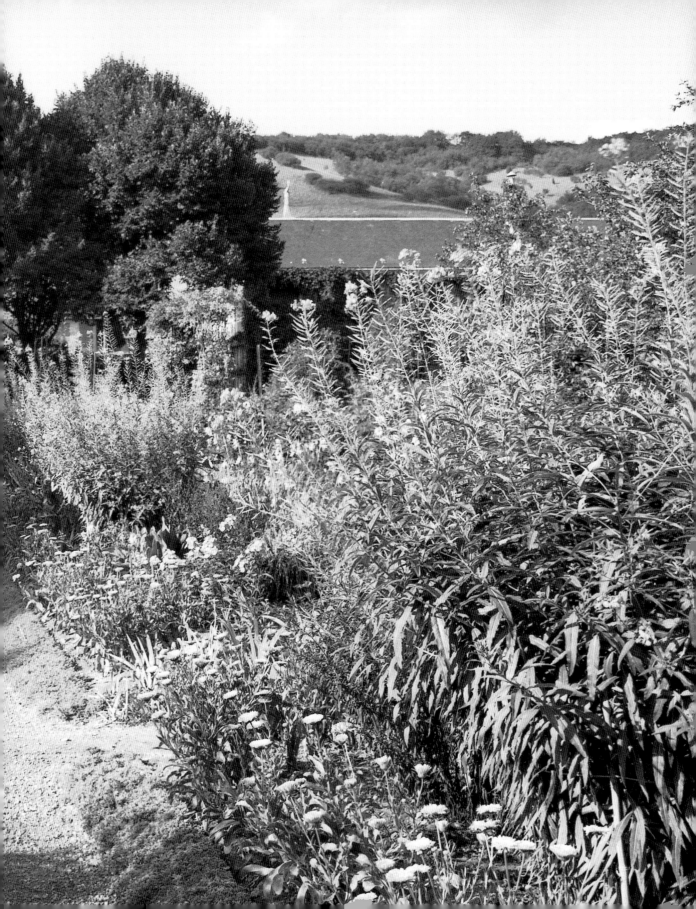

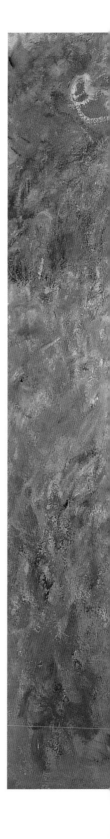

light and dark. Meanwhile, family life at Poissy was evidently disorganized and, despite having been an indolent and truanting pupil himself, Monet wanted to find good schools for all the children. In April of that year, trudging from the village of Vernon along the banks of the Epte near its confluence with the Seine between Paris and Rouen, he found himself enchanted by the springtime exuberance of blossom and wild flowers in the village of Giverny. On an impulse, he enquired about renting a property, and was introduced to Louis Singeot, the owner of a rustic farmhouse with pink stucco walls and an attached barn.

Monet signed the lease at once, doing so regardless of financial anxiety. Merely in order to move his penniless household he had to borrow money, writing for that purpose on 29 April to the art dealer Paul Durand-Ruel. He was to prove both supportive and generous; at the time of the move to Giverny, he lent Monet in total 4,500 francs against future work for removal costs and initial settlement of rent.

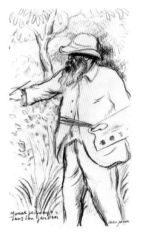

Both Alice Hoschedé and Monet had strong views on the garden at Giverny as they found it on their arrival. One subject of disagreement was the spruce and cypress avenue that formed a key feature.

'… it is **essential** to think **only** about nature; it is by dint of observation and by reflection that you make discoveries.'

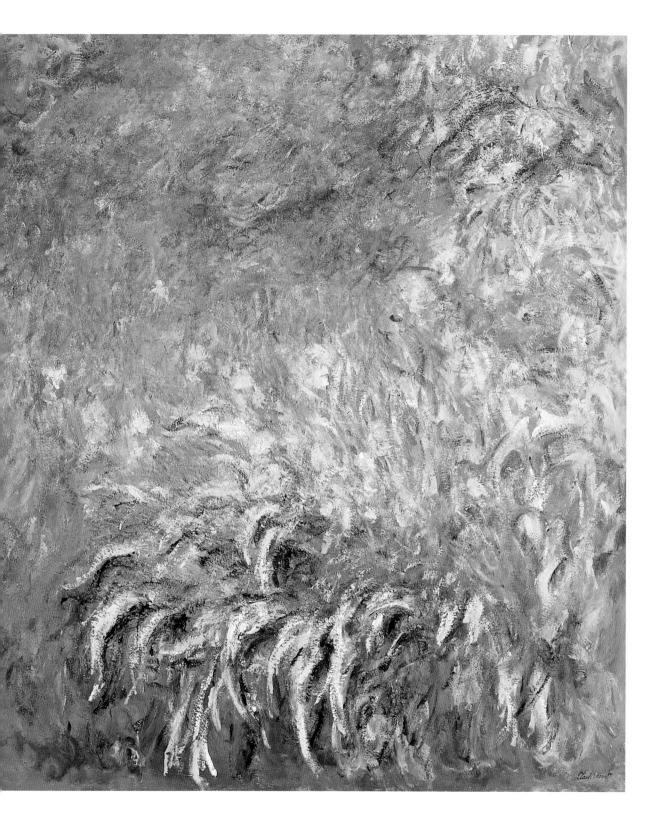

Monet, instantly removing the typical French formal box hedging of the Norman-style potager, also disliked the avenue and planned to destroy this, too. But all his indignation and cajolery failed to persuade Alice, who perhaps felt that this central axis imposed an overall dignity and order. Alice's personal tastes were also met by the flowerbeds immediately around the house. Another concern, soon after their arrival, was to set the family to work getting in the year's vegetables, along with some flowers as a subject to paint when the weather was bad. Monet's first studio was the adjoining barn, which had a beaten earth floor. To this structure he added a doorway leading into the house, and a large window.

It was not easy for Monet's large and unorthodox household to settle in their new location. He and Alice had come to live as man and wife, in a relationship that flouted the mores of the Normandy countryside. Indeed, in the village France itself was viewed by the Givernois as the foreign country over the border. And in such a rural community, to be an artist did not constitute proper work. The Monets' and Hoschedés' manners, clothes, food and family outings all provoked fear of

Right Monet gradually replaced the apple trees at Giverny with frothy-blossomed ornamental Japanese cherry trees. In spring the grass beneath them was enlivened with naturalized daffodils; while in summer the family played and rested in their shade.

'... each minute an ever-changing light transforms

the unknown, and their early years in Giverny were marked by petty acts of unpleasantness. Within Monet's own extended family, his brother Leon would only entertain Monet and his two sons, Jean and Michel. Not surprisingly, the house and its walled garden became a sanctuary for all its inhabitants.

It was, however, during his first years at Giverny that Monet travelled away from home more than at any other time in his life. For months on end he undertook work at new locations introduced to him by friends or family. Meanwhile, he and Alice wrote to each other almost daily. During his travels

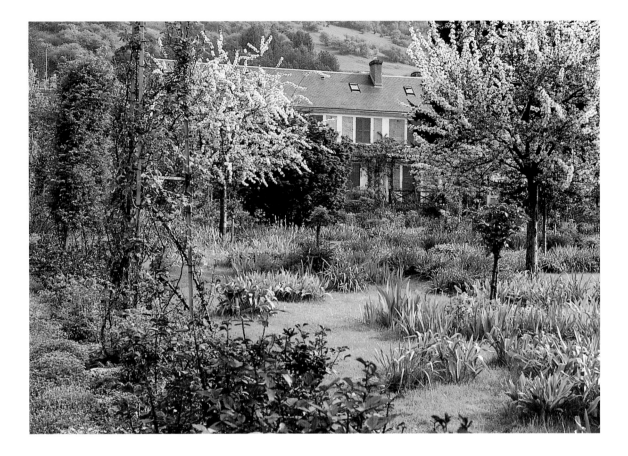

the atmosphere **and the beauty of things.'**

in the 1880s, for example, he advised on her management of domestic details, such as household economies and keeping the teenage boys in check. He also demanded to know why she should want to leave him. One crisis in their relationship produced a particularly tempestuous exchange of letters, of which only Monet's survive, from a time he spent on the Channel coast at Etretat. He wrote, on 9 November 1885: 'How odd it is that while I think of you with such affection and try and show it to you as well as I am able, your thoughts are always at their blackest...'. On 22 February 1886, he

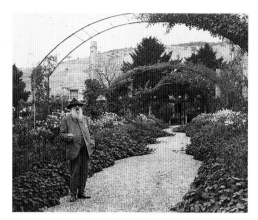

declared: 'You ask me to think things over and come to a decision ... I find it impossible to get used to the idea of a separation ... Anyway, enough of that, I'm very unhappy, really miserable and I haven't the heart to do anything; the painter in me is dead ... that once I've made up my mind to go it alone I'll feel better, you are very much mistaken!' Without thinking of Alice's likely routine, busy at Giverny with eight children, he continues: 'I had a terrible night, thinking of you constantly ... and I hadn't the courage to get out of bed until 10 o'clock ...'. Eventually, Monet's return was to resolve their relationship, which blossomed and deepened into one of happy stability and formed the core of life at Giverny. His letters to Alice, which fortunately she preserved, provide a telling

Left In 1925, the last year of his life, Monet stands in the Grande Allée amid burgeoning cushions of nasturtiums. The iron hoops now familiar to visitors had been put in place around 1920, and the pair of yews and the spruce stumps represented the last vestiges of the original plantings.

'Nature has been a splendid refuge for Monet … an embarrassment of riches that he has seized.'

insight into their relationship; on her death in 1911, Monet was to lock himself away to reread them.

Just three years after the family's arrival at Giverny, in 1886, not only did Monet begin to enjoy a large increase in the sales of his work, but his travels also reflected an upturn in his fortunes. In April and May he returned to Holland to paint the tulip fields, whose swathes of colour inspired him to create similar effects in his own garden. Another expedition took him in September to Belle Ile, off the Brittany coast, where he met the young critic and journalist Gustave Geffroy, who was to become an important visitor to Giverny.

Monet eventually bought the property at Giverny in 1890 for 22,000 francs, paid over three years. Thereafter, the com-

Right The circle closed – revealing the Grande Allée as a verdant tunnel engulfed by plants. The setting sun is mirrored and reflected in the yellow *helianthus*, and the rounded nasturtium leaves seem to float across the gravel path.

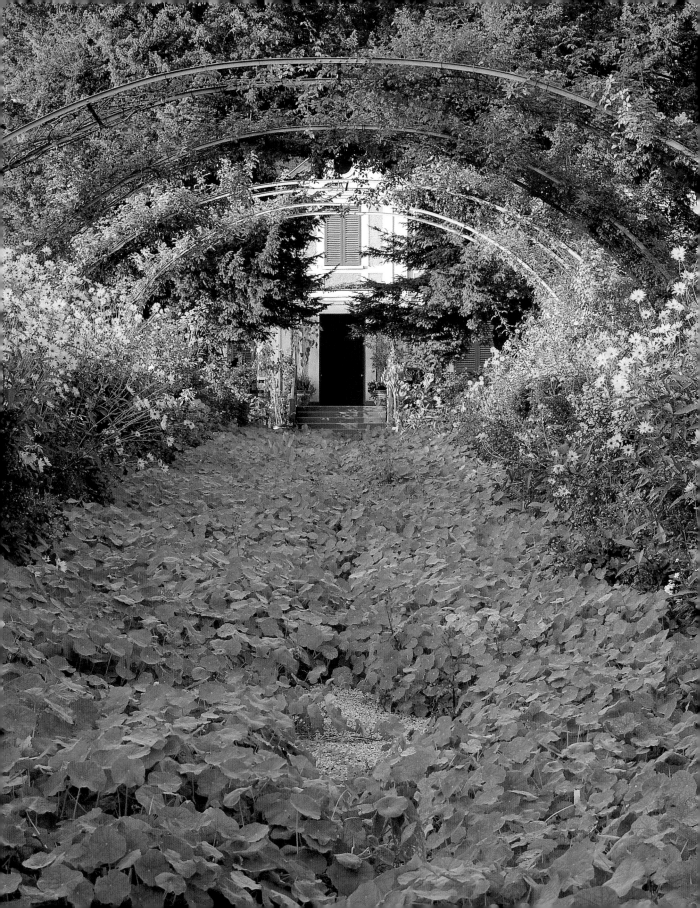

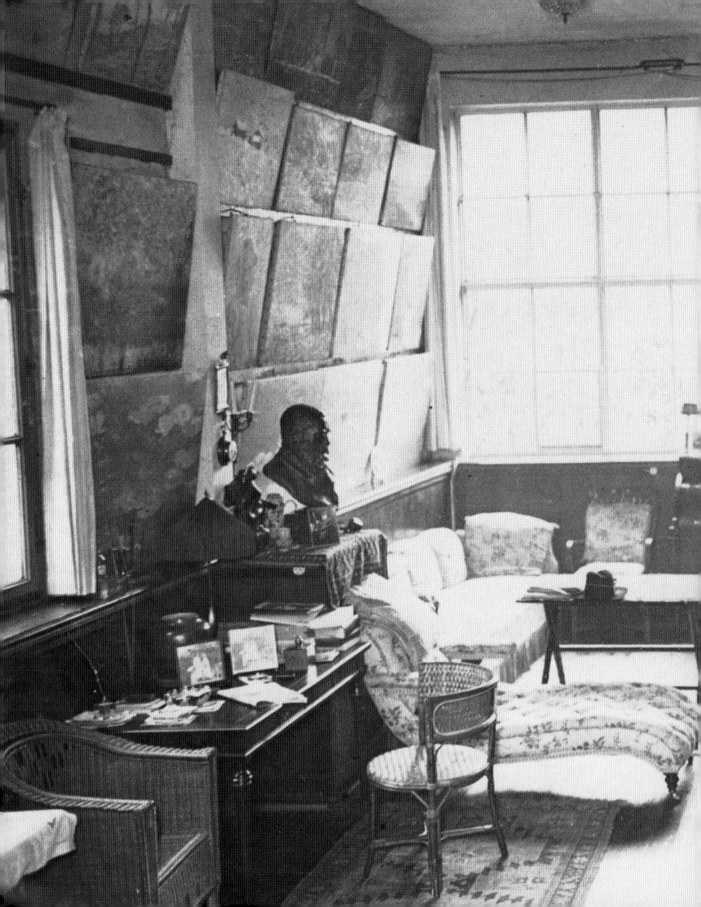

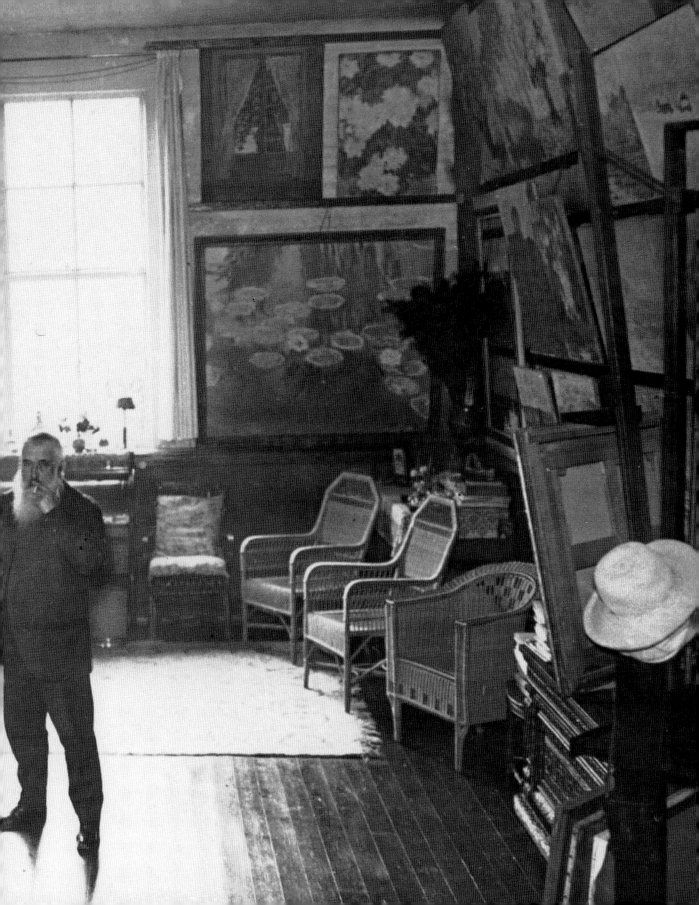

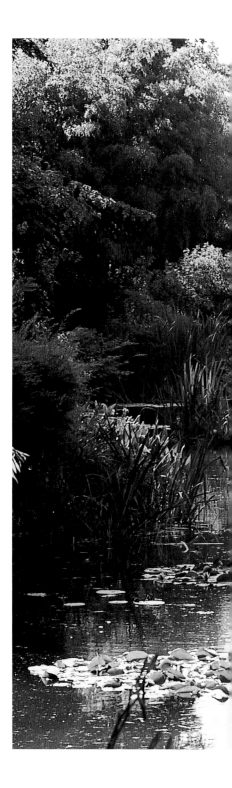

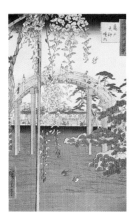

bination of ownership and greatly improved finances encouraged him to renovate and enlarge it. The pink stucco exterior was restored and Monet meticulously supervised the painting of the shutters in a shade of blue-green. The interior was very much Alice's territory; nevertheless, both their personalities are reflected in its décor. In 1893, Jacques-Emile Blanche, painter and friend, described how 'Monet had lined his dining room walls with white damask cloth with Japanese designs on its silvery background'. By October of the same year, new colour schemes included the gloriously sunny yellow of the dining room, the overall effect of which might be described as Vermeer meets Whistler, and which provided a fit setting for Monet's collection of Japanese prints. A small panelled salon painted in blue served as a library for over 600 books. Monet's original studio, already enlarged in 1886, was refitted in 1891, finally becoming the family *salon* in 1897, with its walls displaying a chronology of his works. He would often read aloud here to the family, for whom it was a favourite place to gather together. Upstairs, the south-facing bedrooms overlooked the gardens and the waving poplars beyond. Works here by contemporary artists, many of them

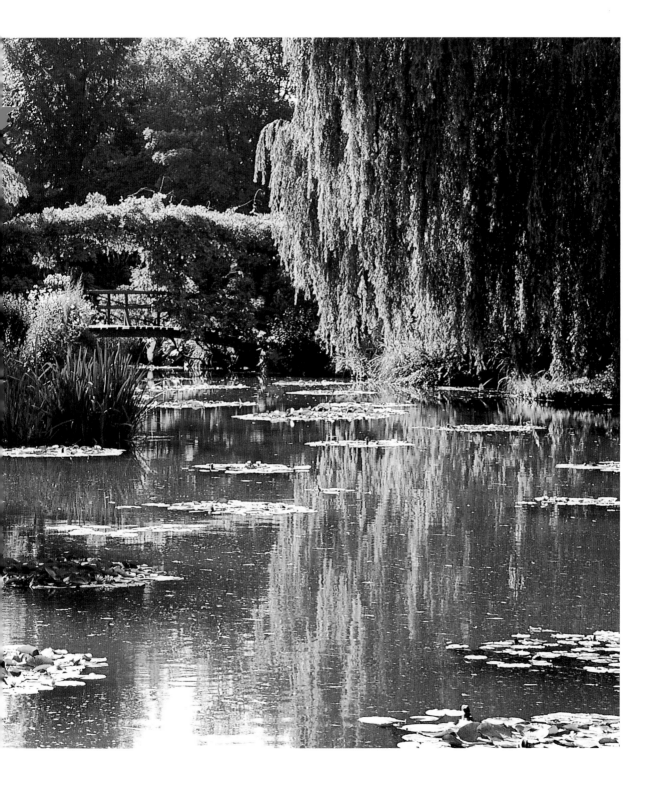

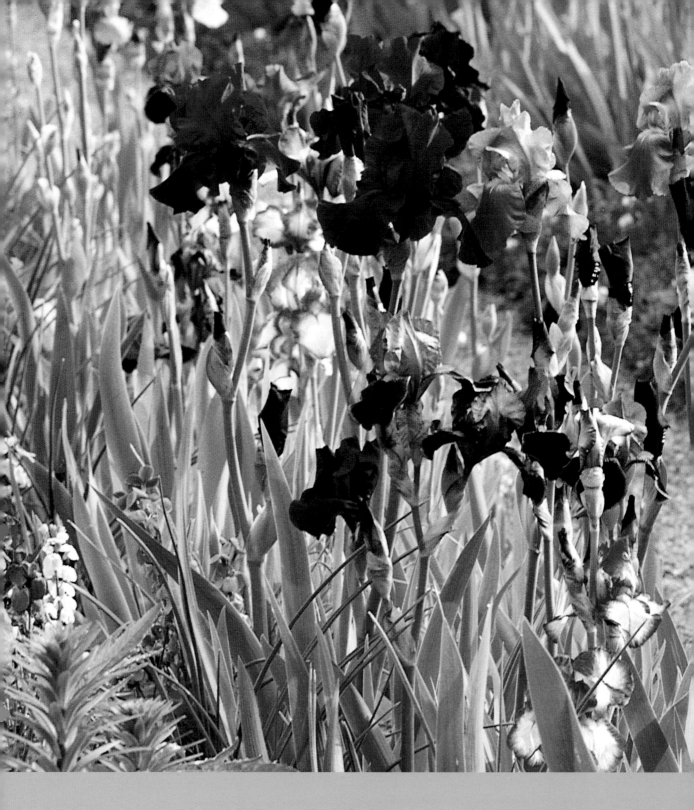

' ... they are so lovely and so

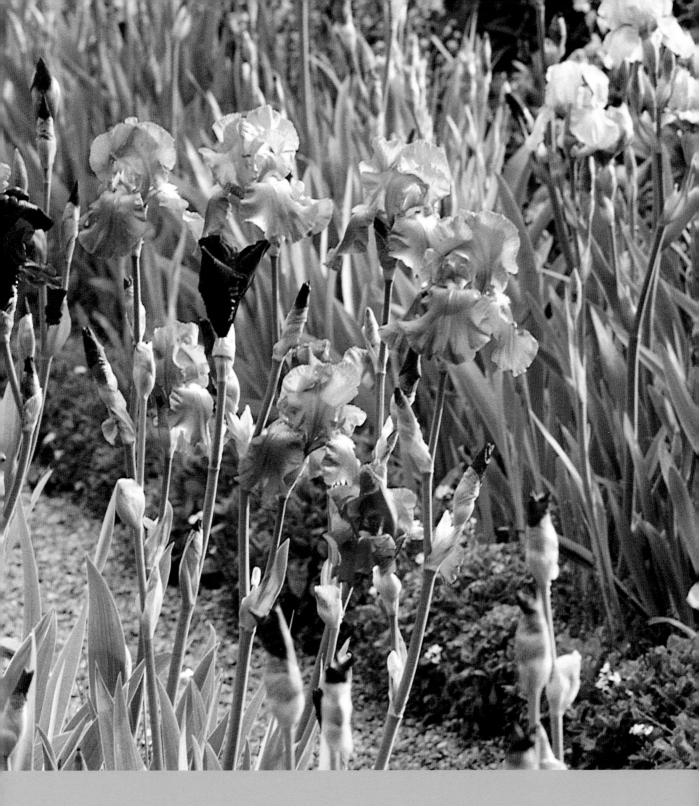

calm, these ordinary flowers.'

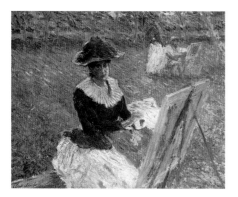

Previous page The architectural accents of iris flowers dominate the exuberant banks of flowers at Giverny.

Left Blanche, the only artist of the younger Hoschedé-Monet generation, is portrayed in **Blanche Hoschedé Painting**, *1890*.

friends, included those of Cézanne, and Renoir, whose *The Mosque, Arab Festival* was bought by Monet in 1900 because it reminded him of his national service in Algeria.

Outside, on nearby Nettle Island, a shed was built to house four boats, including the elderly *atelier-bateau* ('studio boat') used by Monet as a studio further up the Seine at Argenteuil. Alice's son Jean-Pierre recalled a vivid childhood memory of Monet painting his sisters in a small boat on the River Epte, their reflections mingling with the waving river weeds.

It was during his years with Alice – and partly through her influence – that Monet became an avid and eclectic reader. Among the writings of his contemporaries, many of whom were to be his friends, he enjoyed works by the Goncourt brothers, Flaubert, Maupassant, Mirbeau, Zola and the Symbolist poets Mallarmé and Maeterlinck; his reading also included the works of Balzac, Ibsen, Tolstoy, Aristophanes and Tacitus – and of Ruskin, whose newly translated *The Stones of Venice* he studied before visiting the city in the autumn of 1908. He much appreciated Delacroix's *Journal*, published in 1893–5, having long admired him as a leader of the Romantic School. Among gardening books, a favourite was the beautifully illustrated, 26-volume *La Flore des Serres et des Jardins d'Europe*.

Despite a low opinion of critics, Monet subscribed to the

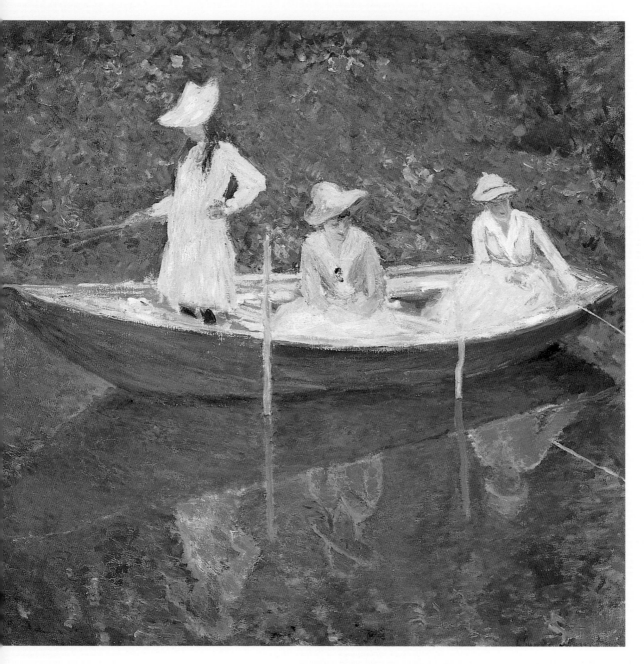

Above The rowing boat or *norvégienne* at Giverny was later transferred to the water garden. ***In the Rowing Boat***, *1887*, shows Germaine, Suzanne and Blanche Hoschedé reflected in still water on a sunny afternoon.

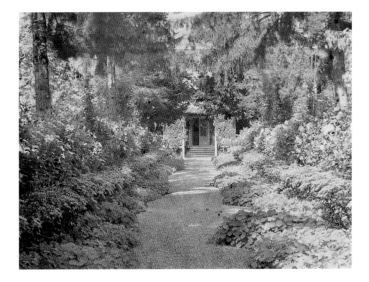

Right A hand-tinted photograph of the well-established Grande Allée. The branches of the spruces create a thick canopy over drifts of plants, and the quality of the photograph gives a bucolic effect – almost as if walking along a high-banked Normandy track.

Parisian cutting agencies La Maison Bonneau and Le Courrier de la Presse, and closely followed the reception of his own work. As well as avidly following current affairs, he subscribed to several horticultural magazines. To enjoy the company of friends and good minds he travelled at least once a month to Paris for dinner at the Café Riche or Les Bons Cosaques. He lunched regularly at the Académie Goncourt, for whose members he also hosted meals at Giverny.

Friends and colleagues

As Monet's prosperity increased, so too did his social circle. Over the years he and Alice welcomed a great variety of people to Giverny, following introductions made through the wider family, fellow artists, dealers and exhibitions of his work. Many of these encounters went on to produce firm friendships, around an inner group of artists with families of similar age, such as Berthe Morisot, Renoir and Pissarro. Morisot, a sister-in-law of Manet, had helped to widen Monet's literary circle by introducing him, with Renoir, to Mallarmé. When in London in 1887, Monet stayed with James McNeill Whistler, whose art greatly impressed him; the following winter he in turn introduced Whistler to Stéphane Mallarmé, who subsequently translated Whistler's lecture 'Ten o'clock'. Octave Mirbeau, an outspoken critic, wrote a number of articles for *La France* praising Monet's work and the introduction to the 1889 retrospective that Monet shared with Auguste Rodin. The enthusiasm with which Mirbeau took to gardening caused Monet and his fellow artist and gardener Gustave Caillebotte much amusement. Rodin was also a guest at Giverny, though his reception there was mixed; on one occasion at dinner he stared so oddly that the girls of the family asked to leave the room; the journalist and statesman Georges Clemenceau, one of Monet's closest friends, described him as stupid, vain and over-fond of money. In November 1894, Mary Cassatt came to visit, bringing with her Paul Cézanne, who was astonished to meet Rodin, as well as Clemenceau and the writer Gustave Geffroy, by now also one of Monet's dearest friends.

On at least three occasions whilst living at Giverny, Monet exerted himself to organize significant aid for one of his friends or for their family. At around the time the Monet family moved house, in 1883, Manet had died, leaving his widow

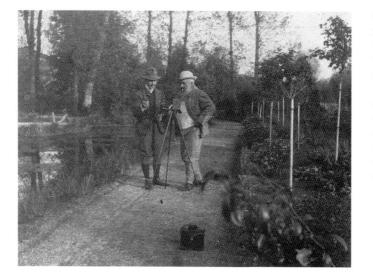

Left Monet with his younger son Michel, a keen photographer, by the banks of the original pool, constructed before 1901. By the turn of the century photography was a recognized artistic medium, popularized by flamboyant leaders such as Nadar, a friend of the Impressionists.

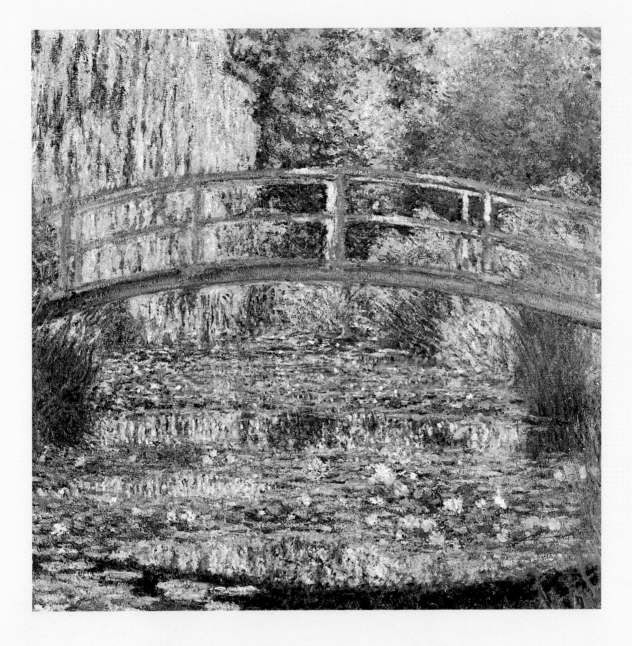

Suzanne with limited means. After the 1889 Grande Exposition in Paris, at which he had enjoyed great success, Monet set up a subscription to purchase Manet's 1863 *Olympia* from Mme Manet for the nation. As a result of this initiative, which almost stopped him painting for a whole year, by February 1890 he had raised

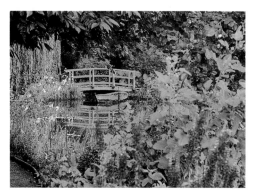

a staggering 19,415 francs. On 7 February he wrote to Armand Fallières, Minister of Public Instruction: 'It is the *Olympia* that we put back in your hands, Monsieur Minister. Our desire is to see it take its place in the Louvre, in its time, among the productions of the French School ...'. Controversy ensued in the press over the suitability of such a painting, but *Olympia* was hung at the Musée du Luxembourg, and in 1907 Clemenceau finally ensured its transferral to the Louvre.

Monet had thus helped Manet's family, both by providing a lump sum and improving the market for his paintings. When Sisley died, on 29 January 1899, Monet also assisted with the family's finances. In an exchange of several letters with Durand-Ruel and Geffroy, on 3 February he wrote: 'I'm going to see about holding a sale for the children's benefit; that's the most urgent thing, then a good exhibition of Sisley's best work should be arranged.' The sale was duly fixed for May.

Monet was also an energetic supporter of Zola throughout the latter's denunciation of the Dreyfus affair. This unpleasant national incident took place in 1894, when Captain Alfred

Left Monet had purchased the Japanese Bridge, which he lined up with the Grande Allée, in 1895. Against convention he painted it green, adding an upper canopy in 1903. Appropriately subtitled 'Harmony in Green', this famous view of **The Water Lily Pond**, *1899*, blurs the definition of land and water for a fluid, challenging effect.

Above Apart from the Japanese Bridge, five smaller bridges span the sluices and the tiny River Ru that feed and maintain the pool. Each carries a meandering path through bamboo and under roses towards a view over fast or slow water, in the manner of a Japanese stroll garden.

'I have **difficulty leaving Giverny**, above all now when I'm arranging the house and garden to my taste.'

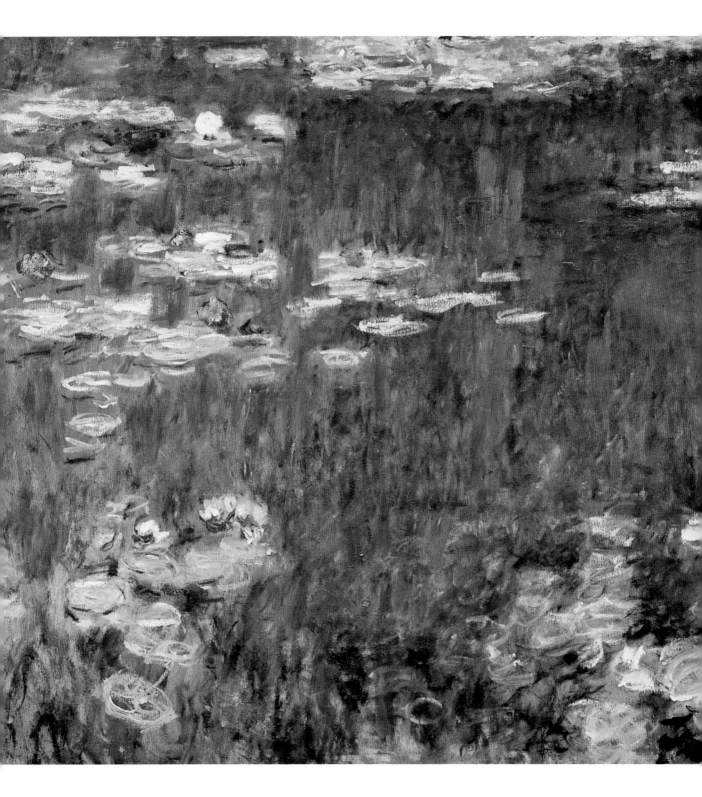

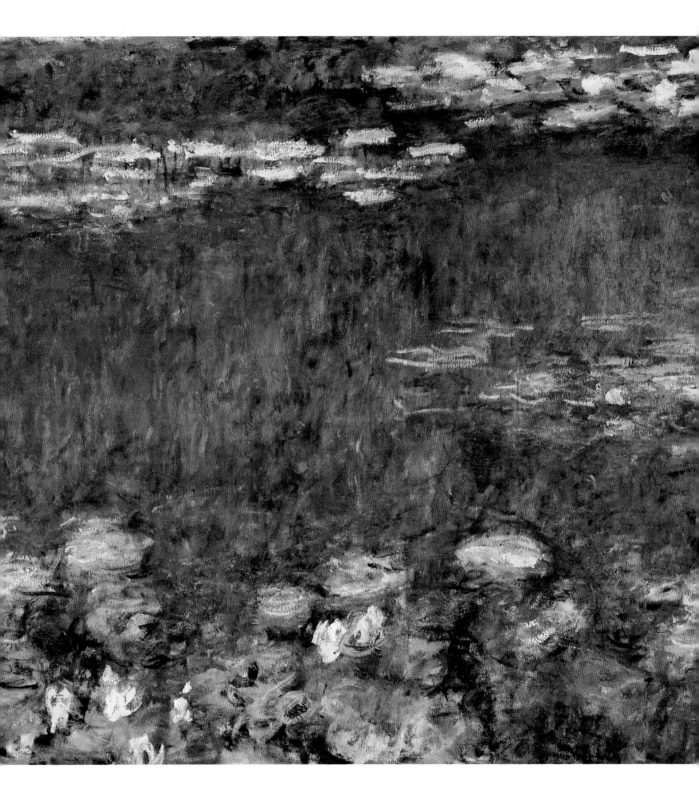

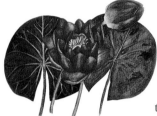

Dreyfus, a Jew, was wrongly accused of passing military secrets to the Germans. He was court-martialled, found guilty of treason, stripped of his rank and exiled on Devil's Island in the Atlantic. In September 1896, his wife requested a retrial, on the grounds that new evidence revealed Charles Esterhazy as the perpetrator. In support of Dreyfus's innocence, Zola contributed two pieces in December 1897 to *Le Figaro*. Monet had not been in contact with Zola since 1886, when he wrote in conditional praise of Zola's book *L'Oeuvre*, which fictionalized the careers of several Impressionists, but he responded to Zola's articles with vigorous approval: 'Bravo and bravo again, for the two fine articles...'. Esterhazy was acquitted, however, and on 13 January 1898 Clemenceau's paper *L'Aurore* published Zola's third and most famous article on the subject, entitled '*J'accuse*', in which he denounced both the military and government. Monet, backed by Pisarro, wrote from Giverny offering his support, and added his name to a 'Manifesto of the Intellectuals'. Amid a nationwide atmosphere of vitriolic anti-Semitism, Zola was convicted of libel and went into exile. In a mood of disgust, Monet left too, for London, in the autumn of 1899, accompanied by Alice and her daughter Germaine. While based at the Savoy Hotel, he started his 'Londons' [*sic*] series

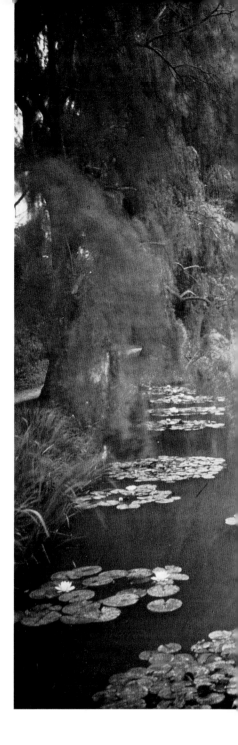

'This house and

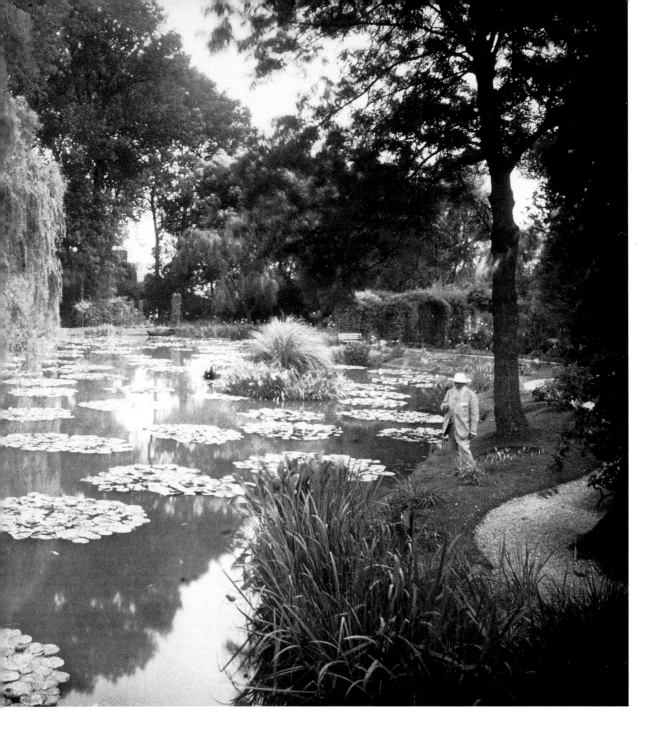

garden is also a work of art, and Monet has put all his
life into creating and perfecting it.'

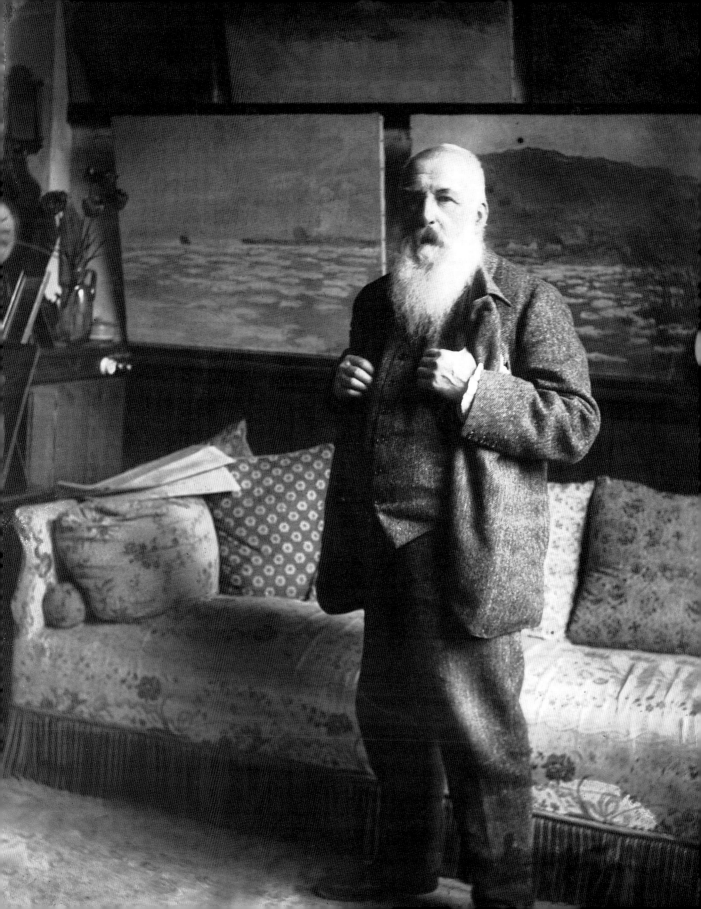

'What can be said of me ... a man who is interested in nothing but his painting? His garden as well, of course, and his flowers, simple ones.'

of paintings and received several visitors, including Clemenceau and Geffroy.

Geffroy had worked as a journalist on *La Justice*, owned and edited by Georges Clemenceau, from its first edition on 14 January 1880. After his first meeting with Monet on Belle Ile in 1886, he had reintroduced him to Clemenceau, whom Monet had known back in the 1860s. Although qualified and formerly practising as a doctor, in the intervening decades Clemenceau had devoted himself to the political pursuit of his ideals of justice, liberty and truth. The energy he brought to this, together with his role in the closing years of World War I as prime minister, was to earn him the nickname 'Le Tigre'. He was vehemently anti-Catholic, an expert on Chinese and Japanese art, and his enthusiasms embraced good food, speed, travel and the study of light effects. After renting a property at nearby Bernouville in 1902, Clemenceau was also to become one of Monet's neighbours. These three men were the closest of friends into old age; Geffroy died just months before Monet, and Clemenceau three years later. In the 1920s, Geffroy and Clemenceau each

Left Monet in the family sitting room, formerly his first studio, at Giverny. In the paintings behind him the ice floes presage his water lily series. Note the pleated lace cuffs of his shirt – a style of dress remembered by his friend Renoir from their student days.

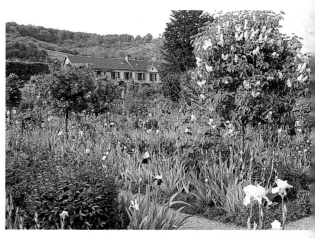

Above The Giverny house glimpsed through a mass of spring flowers from the lower path of the upper garden. In addition to the irises and roses, Monet planted new varieties of lilacs throughout his gardens. These include the double creamy cultivar shown on the right, as well as traditional ones.

wrote an impassioned biography of Monet, in which they eulogized his painting in poetic terms. Far from being sycophantic, their accounts draw the reader into the centre of an exuberant, stimulating milieu, bound together by friendship based on personal affection.

Neighbours and visiting friends at Giverny included a number of Americans – though of these the only artists invited to the Monets' home were Theodore Robinson, Theodore

' ... to ensnare the light, and throw it on to the canvas.'

Butler and Mary Cassatt. Robinson, who established himself in the village in 1885, had been painting two years earlier in the forest of Fontainebleau when a friend took him to meet Monet. Other Americans, arriving by chance, were delighted to discover that Monet lived in Giverny; they included Stanton Young, a first-class tennis player who set about organizing tournaments, and the Perry household, of whom Mrs Lila Cabot Perry, like Young, was also an artist. In due course, the proprietors of the village store and bar, Lucien and Angelina Baudy, responded to an influx of visitors by converting their house into the Hôtel Baudy, complete with an *atelier* in its gardens.

Right Suzanne Hoschedé was Monet's favourite stepdaughter and model. She was 18 in 1886 when he painted this portrait, **Study of a Figure Outdoors Facing Left**, for which he made her pose for so long that she fainted. It is argued that, after her death, her drifting shape was recalled in some of Monet's water lily paintings.

The Monet-Hoschedé ménage

Despite the perceived irregularity of her relationship with Monet, Alice was deeply conventional in her faith and upbringing and in that of her children. It was not until the death of Ernest Hoschedé, in 1891, that the couple were free to marry. Meanwhile, she returned to nurse Hoschedé in the weeks before he died, and he is buried in the family grave at Giverny. She and Monet had a feeling for family unity that led them both to resist anyone or anything that might threaten that ideal, including their children's suitors. Certainly no step-

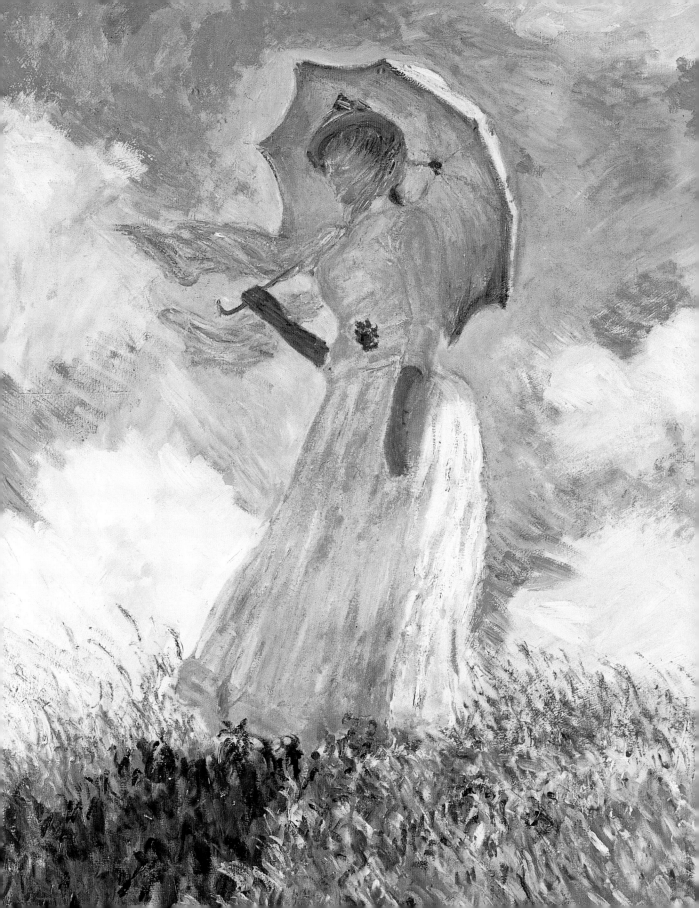

daughter of Monet was welcome to marry an artist – Blanche, for example, experienced his wrath as her relationship with struggling artist John Leslie Breck was broken up.

The only artist among her siblings, Blanche finally married her step-brother Jean in 1897. An apartment for them at Giverny was incorporated into the newly constructed second studio, a large building that flanked the northern boundary of the garden with north-facing windows in the roof and wall and south-facing windows overlooking greenhouses and the meadows beyond.

Within the intense, almost claustrophobic life of the family the fortunes of the siblings varied. Michel Monet and Jean-Pierre Hoschedé effectively spent their whole lives at Giverny. As young boys they were fascinated by the local flora: Jean Pierre and the parish priest, Abbé Anatole Toussaint, went on to publish *La Flore de Vernon et de la Roche Guyon* in 1898. Sadly, though, Michel was to lose this interest; when I asked why one can read only of Michel's safaris and fast cars, I was told that this was all he did with his life.

Jean Monet trained in Switzerland as a chemist, before working with his uncle in Rouen, but after Alice's death he and Blanche returned to the apartment at Giverny. A decline in his health left him increasingly incapacitated, at first physically, then also mentally. Blanche devotedly nursed him until his death in 1914. Of the Hoschedé boys, Jacques married and moved to Norway, where Monet visited him in the course of a painting expedition in 1895. Jean-Pierre lived independently but maintained an active interest in Giverny and in Monet's work; his *Monet, ce mal connu* (1960) offers a fascinating fly-on-the-wall portrait of his step-father.

The first of Monet and Alice's combined offspring to

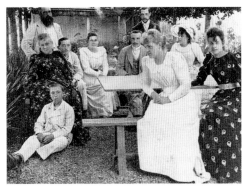

Above The Monet-Hoschedé family shown in the garden at Giverny in the late 1880s. From left to right: Michel Monet, Alice Hoschedé, Jean-Pierre Hoschedé, Blanche Hoschedé, Jean Monet, Jacques Hoschedé, Germaine Hoschedé, Suzanne Hoschedé and Marthe Hoschedé. Suzanne is particularly distinctive in her patterned dress.

Right Monet would sit for hours by his pool contemplating the reflections of sky and clouds that inspired such works as **Water Lilies**, 1908. The four rare and expensive red water lilies, bought in 1904, were by now well established.

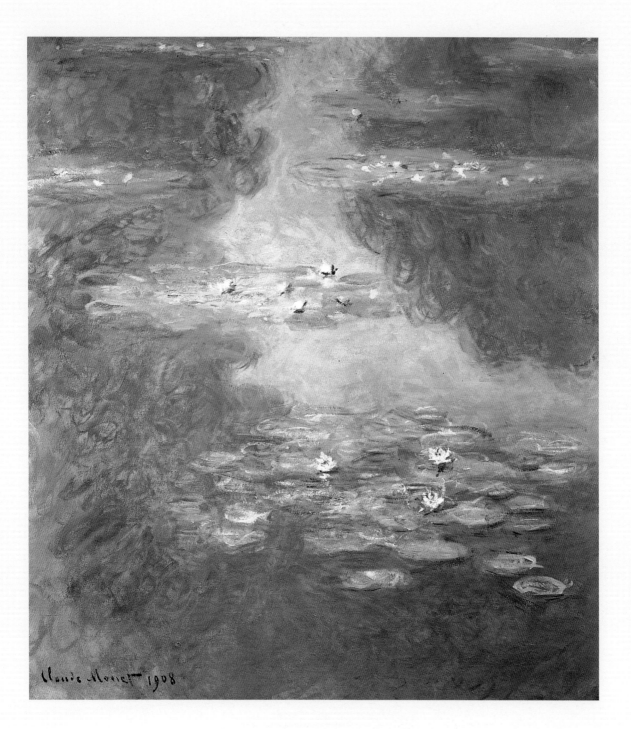

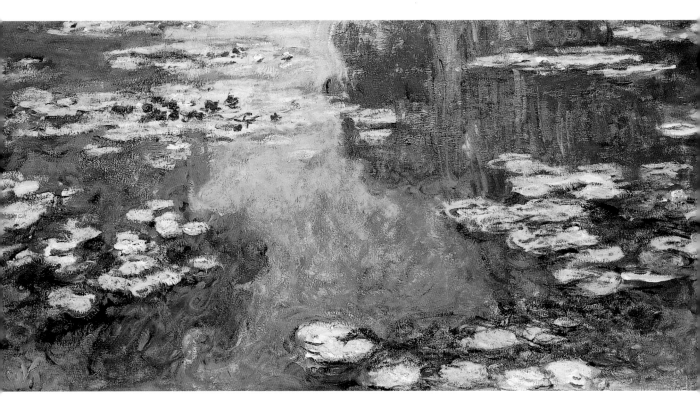

Above In addition to the *Grandes Décorations*, Monet produced many other 'Water Lily' paintings reflecting the different moods of light and season. **Water Lilies**, *1918-19,* reveals a complex mixture of green and yellow foliage and shadow, hinting at hidden depths.

marry was Suzanne, who surmounted much initial opposition to her choice of the artist Theodore Butler, a friend of John Singer Sargent. Her wedding, on 20 July 1892, was delayed in order that on 16 July Monet could finally marry Alice, enabling him to give Suzanne away as her legal stepfather. Suzanne had been Monet's favourite model; one portrait, illustrating his hopes that she might marry his son, Jean, depicts them in the orchard at Giverny in the spring of 1886.

In *Woman with a Parasol*, also painted in 1886, Monet was startled at Suzanne's physical resemblance to his portrait of Camille with Jean, executed a decade earlier. In paintings and photographs alike, Suzanne's image exudes a certain vivacity. However, unlike the clear features and insouciant eyes of Camille in her early portraits, Suzanne's face is almost as if

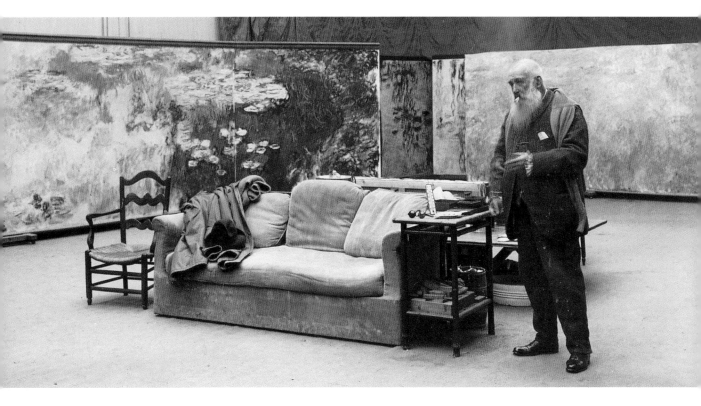

behind gauze. A variety of dates between 1889 and 1891 are suggested for the uncharacteristic, almost Symbolist, portrait of Suzanne that was to be Monet's last figure painting. Her face looms clear from a background of spectral gloom, surrounded by three large sunflowers in a vase, but the depiction of her body is subdued. Camille, in her later portraits, had seemed to fade from sight, until in the year of her death she appeared to be no more than a shadow on a background of lilacs. Suzanne was destined tragically to replicate Camille's fate; when she died, on 6 February 1899, she had been paralysed since 1894, following the birth of her daughter Lily. Her children were cared for by her sister Marthe, who married Butler in 1900.

Germaine Hoschedé, despite initial attraction to Alfred

Above The vast third studio was over 276 m (905 sq ft) and cost over 35,000 francs. Practical but unattractive, the building embarassed Monet by its hideous bulk, but it was an invaluable home for the *Grandes Décorations* canvases. Northern light filled the interior, to which he brought the garden in painted form.

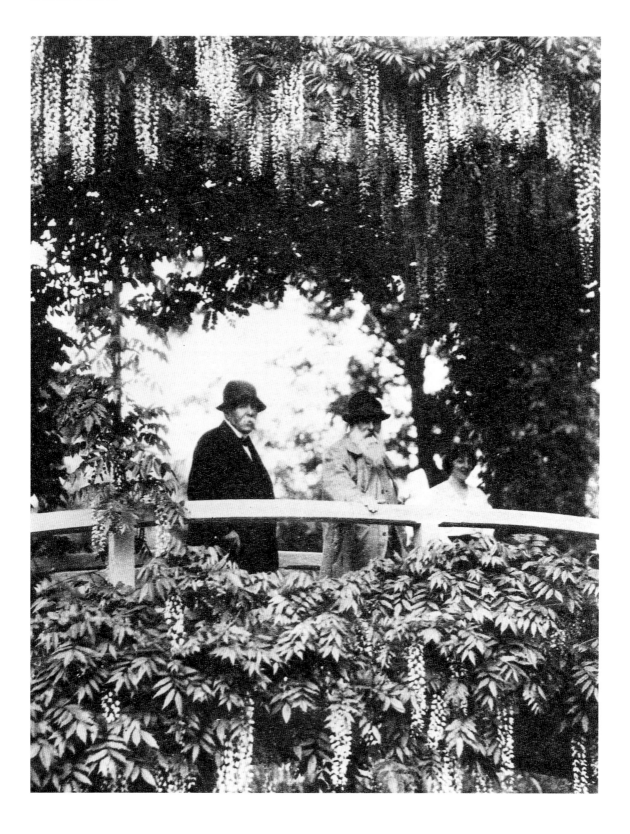

Sisley's son Pierre – another match that was viewed as unsuitable – married Albert Salerou, a Monaco lawyer at Giverny in 1902. The garden, in four photographic views, featured on the menu for the wedding breakfast. Albert and Germaine's daughter Simone returned to Giverny to marry in 1926, just four months before Monet's death; the luncheon menu was likewise headed with views of the garden.

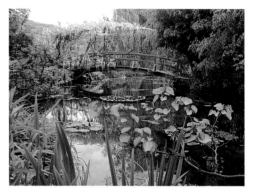

Above The white wisteria blooms on top of the Japanese Bridge bask in light. When Monet painted his first water garden pictures from this angle, the pool was a third of the size shown here and the bridge was a plain arc.

The last decade

After Jean Monet's tragic and prolonged death, Blanche, who had forsaken her own prospects as a painter, lived at Giverny as housekeeper and muse to Monet – his *ange bleu*, as Clemenceau described her. With the outbreak in that year of World War I, Monet refused to leave his domain. He turned his energies to producing fruit and vegetables for the nearest field hospitals from his walled plot at the Maison Bleue in the Rue du Chêne, Giverny, which he had bought a few years before in order to have a separate kitchen garden. Another late acquisition was a third studio, built in 1916 at a cost greater than the whole property's original purchase price. It is

' ... the wisteria has never been lovelier ... in this heat it won't last. '

a hideous monolith, the unattractive bulk of which embarrassed Monet, but it was vast enough for him to use it to paint his commemorative *Grandes Décorations* project after the war.

Throughout the war, Giverny remained an oasis, unaffected by the human catastrophe taking place beyond its walls. It became a sanctuary away from war work for Clemenceau, who wrote to Monet and visited whenever he could snatch an

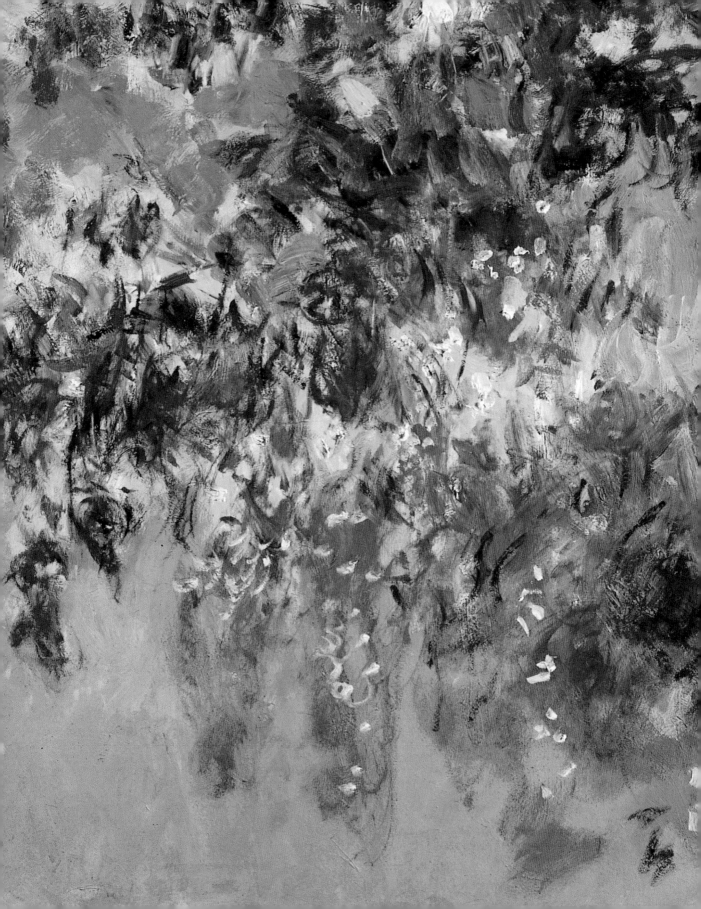

hour or two. During these years, the very private doors to
Monet's garden were publicly opened just once, in 1915, for a
film by Sasha Guitry featuring France's leading cultural figures. Monet felt that by being filmed in the act of painting he
was contributing to the war effort.

On 18 November 1919, having been prime minister since
1917, Clemenceau took his first day off in years and travelled
with Geffroy to Giverny to view the two water lily panels that

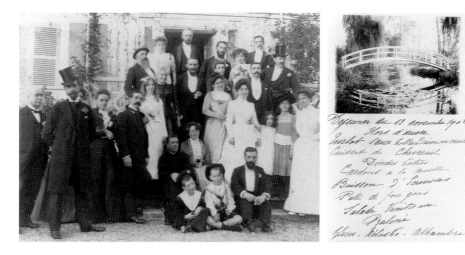

Monet wished to give the nation as a celebration of France's
victory. However, Clemenceau saw the recently executed
weeping willow paintings and considered them an apt embod-
iment of torment tempered with triumph; he asked for one
water lily painting and one weeping willow picture. These
panels would expand into a sequence that filled two elliptical
rooms and encapsulated Monet's overall vision of his lily pool.
It was an undertaking that filled the last seven years of his life.

By the time he reached old age, Monet's financial shrewd-
ness had helped to make him immensely rich. His income in
1899 had been 227,000 francs; in 1901 he sold 17 canvases,
which realized 127,500 francs; in 1912 his paintings brought
an income of 369,000 francs. He took excellent financial
advice, so that in 1903 his investments allowed him not to be

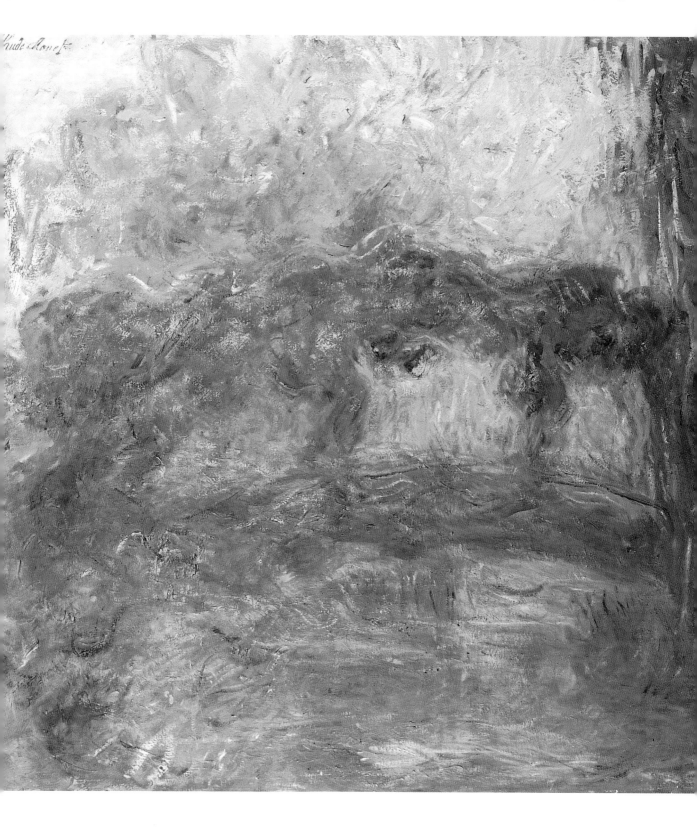

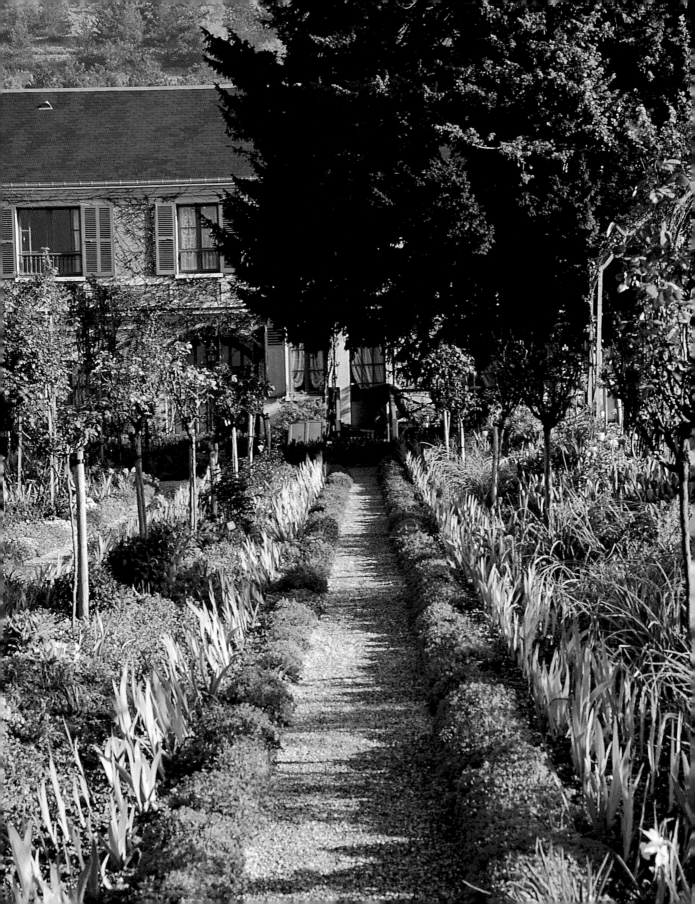

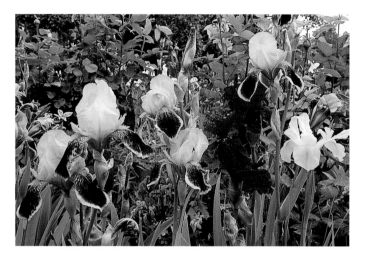

obliged to sell any paintings at all. By 1919, his securities amounted to an impressive 1,000,000 francs, yielding 40,000 francs per annum in interest alone.

Despite this wealth Monet would fail, unforgivably, to leave any provision for Blanche – yet he ended his life amidst the love of his step-daughter and that of Clemenceau and Geffroy. Goodness, friendship and humour are apparent throughout the accounts of these years, with never a trace of martyrdom. Surely they all reached moments when they must have loved more than liked the thoroughly irascible and impossible Monet, who would rage against the inadequacies of advancing age in a way that was best soothed by cajoling him into a calming contemplation of his gardens.

In time it was only the house and gardens at Giverny that gave the welcome face that Monet himself could no longer always offer. Within its walls he became solitary, deliberately cut off from the unrecognizable world without, spending hours in contemplation of the garden – especially the effects of light across the surface of his pool. In 1921, Geffroy wrote that Monet survived because of an inner strength which was like an invincible force animated by his burning artistic desires. Photographs show him increasingly as sporting a

Left The raised carp's-
back beds of the
Grande Allée are lined
with parallel straight
paths edged by drifts
of aubretia. Contrasting
vertical accents are
provided by emerging
irises and rose trees.

'The distortion and
exaggeration of colours
I see is quite terrifying …
If I were condemned to
seeing nature always as
I see it now, I'd prefer
to stay blind and just
remember the beauties
I have always seen.'

Right During Monet's lifetime this painting, **The House**, **Giverny**, *c.1922*, remained in his studio without being exhibited. It shows the impact of developing cataracts on his sense of colour balance and perception. Many of his canvases painted at this time were dominated either by strong reds and yellows or cooler greens and blues.

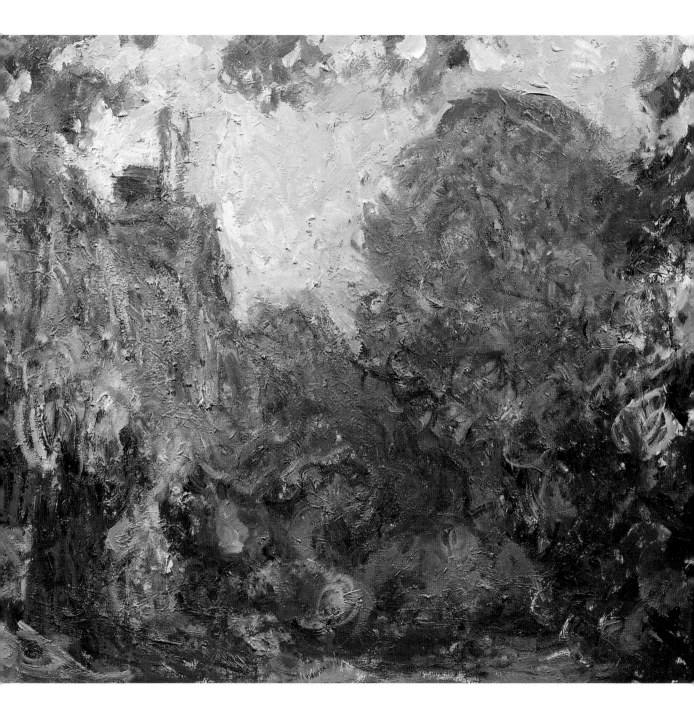

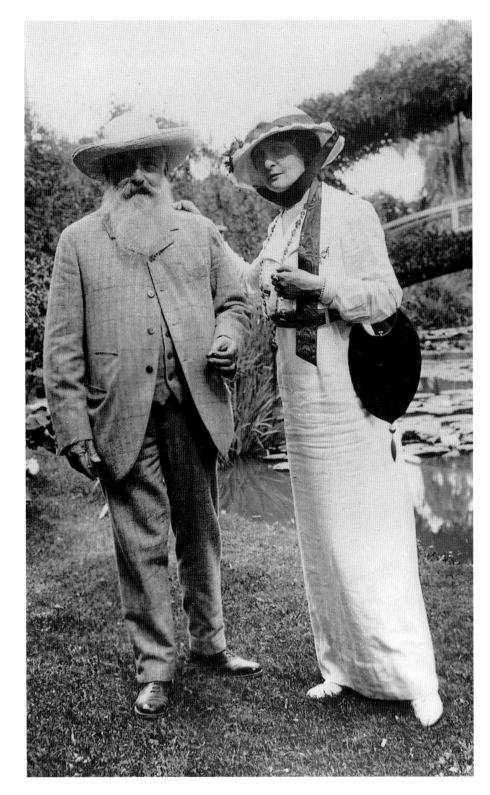

Right Marguerite
Namara, the American
opera singer, photo-
graphed with Monet
during a visit to Giverny
in 1913. She sang for
the artist in the third
studio, surrounded by
water lily canvases.

broad-brimmed straw hat to protect his eyes from the intensity of the light. His last years were tormented by the need to decide whether or not to have an operation that would remove his cataracts. It was not just the operation that daunted him, but the possible after-effects. Nonetheless, the cataract operation was carried out and proved successful.

Family photographs had captured light and joy in the new generations who played in the garden during the years when Monet painted and Alice reigned as matriarch. Alice's death in 1911 came as a devasting blow to the whole family; she had been a superb hostess and an exemplary mother, wife and stepmother. Alice's spirit as hostess lived on in a delightful episode in 1913, when Monet entertained Chicago Opera singer Marguerite Namara. Rodin had brought Isadora Duncan to dance before Monet's water lilies in the vast third studio, so Namara insisted on singing for him by the paintings. Theodore Butler duly arranged for his piano to be transported to accompany the performance. In the photograph taken to mark the occasion, the body language speaks volumes. Monet seems to twinkle at the camera; Namara, smiling beatifically, rests a solicitous yet proprietorial hand on his shoulder.

Monet died at Giverny on 5 December 1926, his garden safely bedded down for winter after years of loving care. He had been a truly sensual man whose prodigious taste for bright colours, good food and fast cars was balanced by an exquisite sensitivity to water, light and new life.

Below (top) Suzanne, Germaine and Blanche Hoschedé with Monet in the 1880s. The upper terrace has been softened by cushions of low-growing plants and the attractive blue and white delft *jardiniere* in the foreground.

Below (bottom) The little birthday girl, Sizi Salerou, sits on the steps next to her step-grandfather Monet and her cousin Lily Butler, *c*.1905. Several birthday photographs were taken in the garden with the extended Monet family.

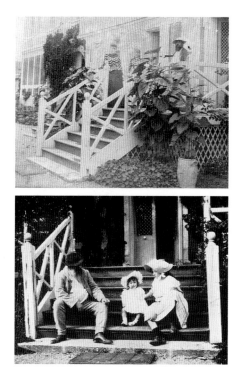

'Monet's garden stands amongst his masterpieces, casting the spell that changes nature into painted works of artistic light.'

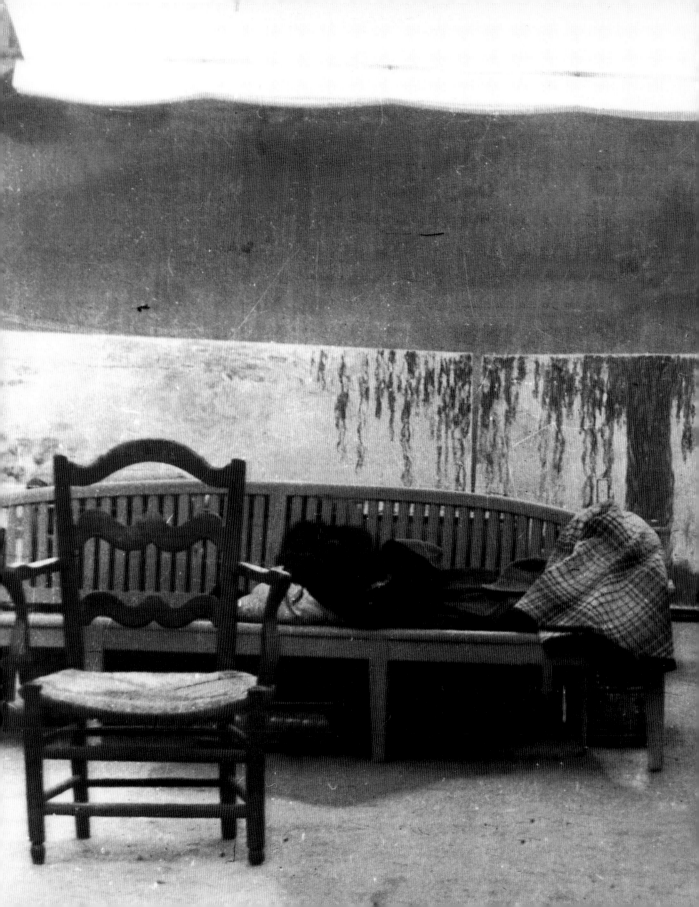

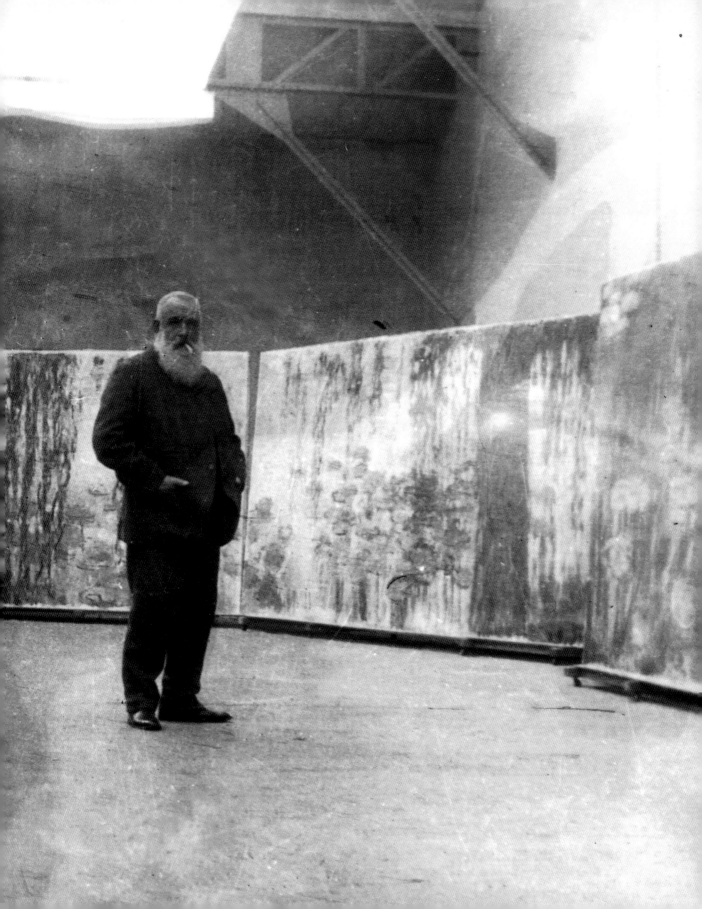

'I am chasing a dream, I want the unattainable. Other artists paint a bridge, a house, a boat; and that's the end. They've finished. I want to paint the air which surrounds the bridge, the house, the boat; the beauty of the air in which these objects are located; and that is nothing short of impossible. If only I could satisfy myself with what is possible!'

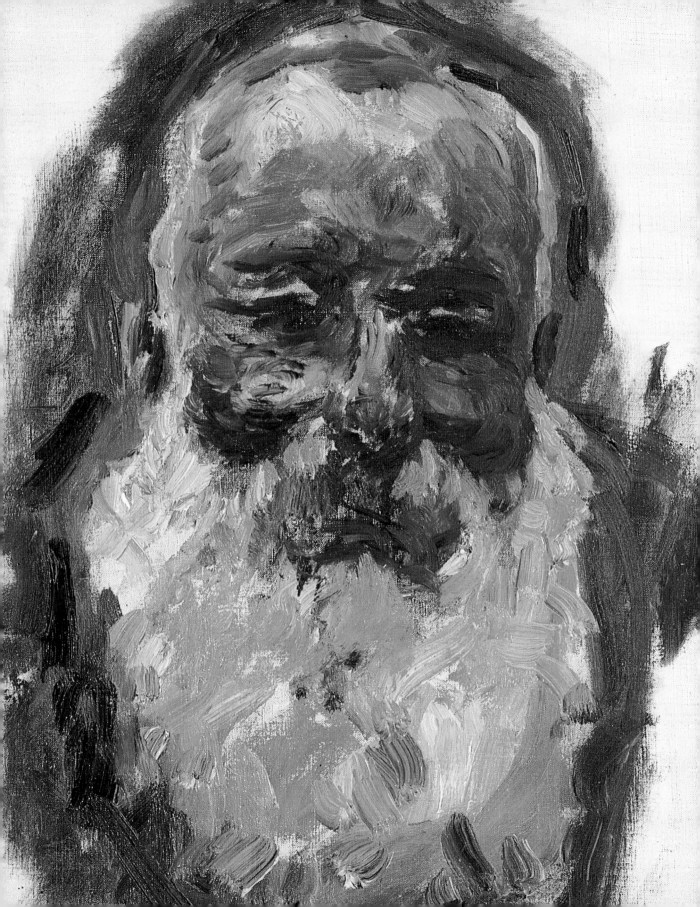

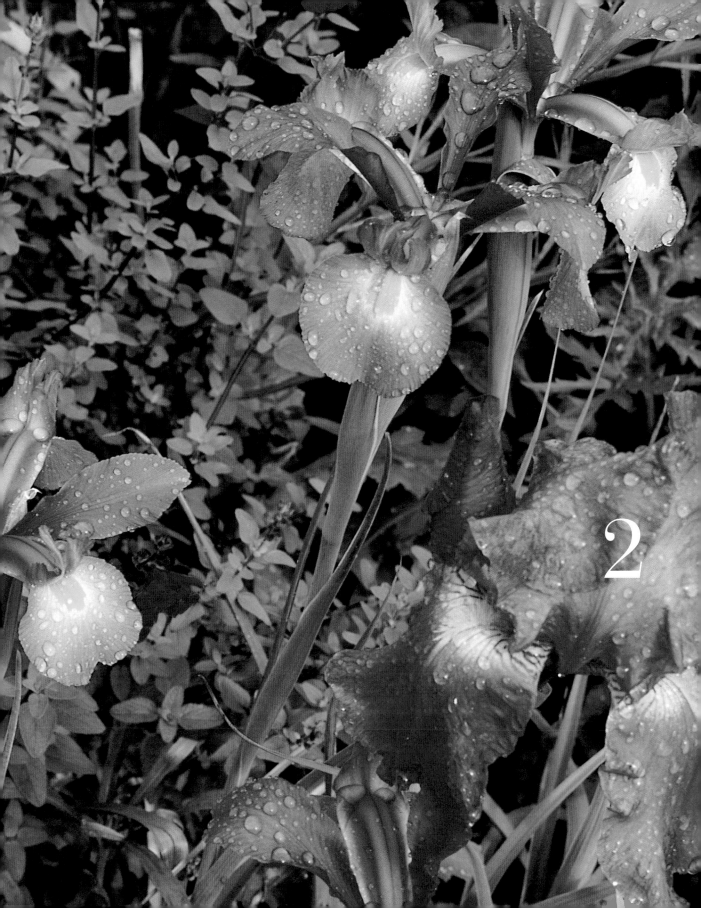

The Garden

Shaping the domain

THERE ARE THREE things to consider in choosing a house and garden – position, position and position. The village of Giverny nestles into a line of low, south-facing hills with a view through quivering poplars to the valley of the Seine and the steep banks beyond the river. Monet's house and the buildings he later added stand along the village street. A veranda on the south front, also built by him, provides a canopied transition from the house into the one hectare (2.5 acre) garden, the sight of which, as Monet first gazed out across his new domain, made him declare himself to be filled with wonder.

The baroque landscapes created for the French court by André Le Nôtre served to symbolize national power and prestige. They provided patriotic inspiration at the end of the 19th century for a country demoralized by crushing defeat in the Franco-Prussian War of 1870. Restorations were undertaken by Henri Duchêne and newly designed gardens traced out in dwarf box, although many of the gardens were distant echoes of the drama and symmetry of the originals. Monet disliked the dreary horticultural layouts that his English contemporary William Robinson was to dismiss as 'pastry-cook gardening'.

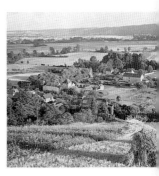

Above The village of Giverny is protected by steep hills with a southern aspect. They fall away towards Monet's beloved Seine valley across a patchwork of trees, fields and meadows.

Right In the 1920s the old friends, Monet and Clemenceau, met whenever possible to take a mandatory stroll around the gardens at Giverny. Following the loss and destruction of World War I, they shared a delight in the changing seasons and the regenerative powers of nature.

Below The house at Giverny is surrounded by billowing flowers. The veranda canopy provides a framework up which the rose 'Mermaid' could climb, to flower under Monet's bedroom window.

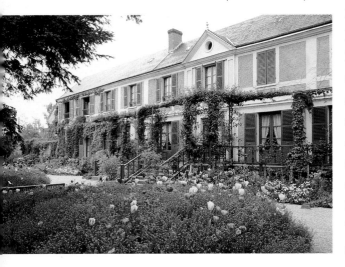

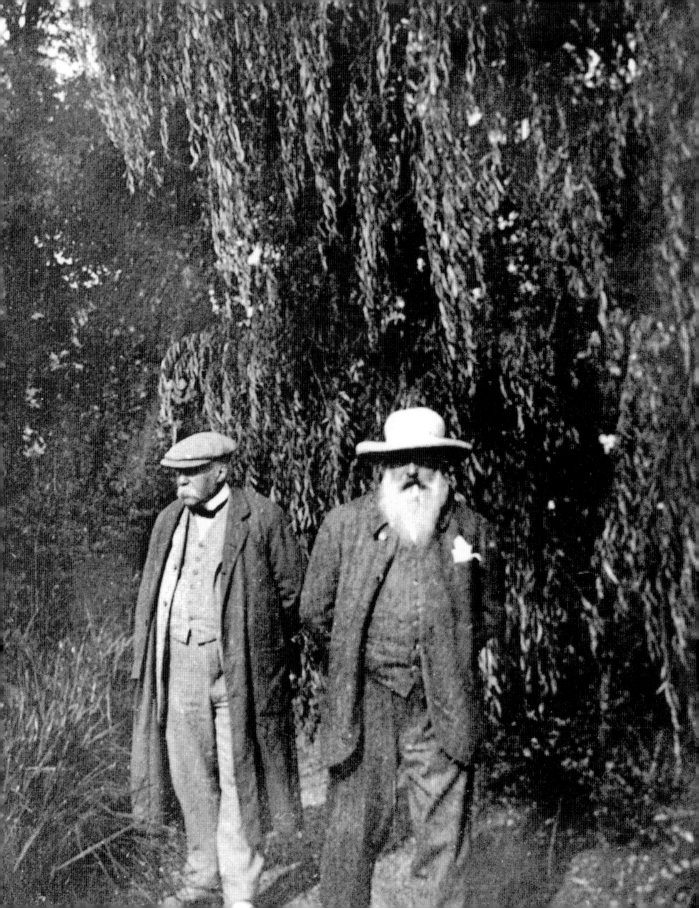

Nonetheless, despite totally different outcomes in their gardens, Monet and Le Nôtre shared the sense of landscape known by the baroque term *pourtraiture* – an exposing or bringing forth, by removing irregularities or accidents of nature, of the essential reality underlying all things.

Le Nôtre's consummate skill had revealed itself in a mastery of perspective. This he characteristically manipulated by varying the distances between the cross axes of his designs, using dramatic effects of light, filtered or reflected by trees,

Right A longer view of the Grand Allée at Giverny. The change in perspective emphasizes the long edgings which appear like ribbons, holding the mass of taller plants behind.

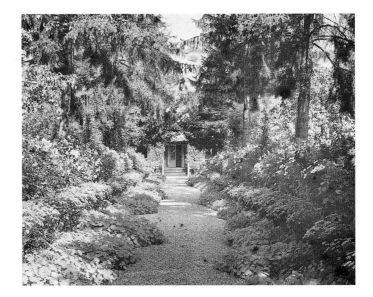

hedges, pools and fountains, to create landscapes that symbolized power. In his hands, the garden became a geometric extension of the house, with long straight avenues and spacious embroidered parterres designed to give a visual release.

Monet was also swift to remove irregularities from his garden at Giverny, whether natural or manmade. However, his manipulation of perspective was taken to such an extreme that in the water garden he excluded it altogether, in favour of revealing the underlying nature through a painterly use of plants. In the upper part of the garden, Monet took an existing central axis and created around it a pattern of rectangular beds that blazed in a vertical and horizontal release of light and colour. Just as he avoided using dark primed canvas, so his planting concealed the garden's well-husbanded soil. This horticultural priming took the form of low cushioning plants, to which was added the rich weave of hooks and dashes of floral colour. West-facing beds were planted with yellow, orange and red flowers whose colours would glow brighter yet in the setting sun. In areas of shade beneath shrubs and trees, Monet established patches of blue flowers in a manner remi-

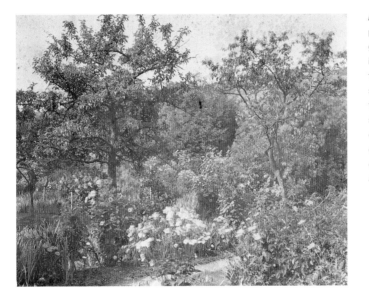

Left A hand-tinted photograph of the gardens at Giverny illustrates the seasonal transition from spring to summer. Blossom, now fading on the trees, is succeeded by a dappled green canopy of leaves above an array of herbaceous and annual plantings.

niscent of his earliest paintings. Picturesque composition – an arrangement of foreground, middle distance and background – was a practice Monet avoided; instead he worked with the *sensation* of nature. In his paintings, he tried to weave foreground and background into a single pictorial effect. Likewise in garden design, he depended on coaxing an explicitly 'natural' response from his plants, allowing annuals such as poppies and verbascum to self-seed at random. In the water garden he worked to decorate the surface of the pool with coloured water lilies and render it a mirror reflecting its carefully wrought surroundings. In 1926, at the end of his life,

Monet declared that when painting he had always 'attached great importance to design and to each work's layout'. In the formal layout of the upper garden at Giverny and the asymmetry of his water garden, here too he applied the same principle, in a composition that stands as testimony to his instinct for design and his attention to detail.

The artist gardener

Monet's first essays in horticulture had been at Ville d'Avray, and subsequent paintings both by him and by his friends Manet and Renoir captured the pretty gardens he created at Argenteuil and Vétheuil. One of his earliest related purchases had been the large blue and white delft *jardinières*, which can be glimpsed in his paintings of Argenteuil in the 1870s and Vétheuil in 1881 and which later adorned the veranda at Giverny. When he moved into the Maison du Pressoir at Giverny it had been a cider farm surrounded by apple orchards. In its garden, a central path passed between a pair of yews and was then lined with alternating cypress and spruce. The flowerbeds by the house, like the divisions of the Norman-style potager, were hedged with dwarf box. Six pleached limes led to an exit on the west side, and to the potager. Monet painted some pictures of the garden's geometric layout, proving his mastery of formal perspective if he chose to use it, but was swift to remove the box hedging that he disliked. He retained the lime trees and planted the flowerbeds by the house with roses, bright geraniums, pinks and annuals. Alice, however, liked the avenue of cypress and spruce, which she felt created an elegant effect, and refused to let it be removed. Her youngest son, Jean-Pierre, recalled that spectacular rows ensued, on what he described as a domestic battleground. A disgruntled compromise was reached, in which Monet removed the cypress and shaved the trunks of the spruce. He then softened the outlines of the surviving trees

Right While the newly extended water garden was maturing, Monet turned to painting his first pictures of the upper garden. Glorious displays of massed irises run parallel to the Grand Allée in this visual celebration of ***The Artist's Garden at Giverny**, 1900.*

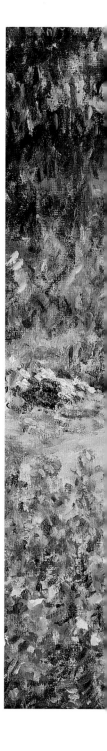

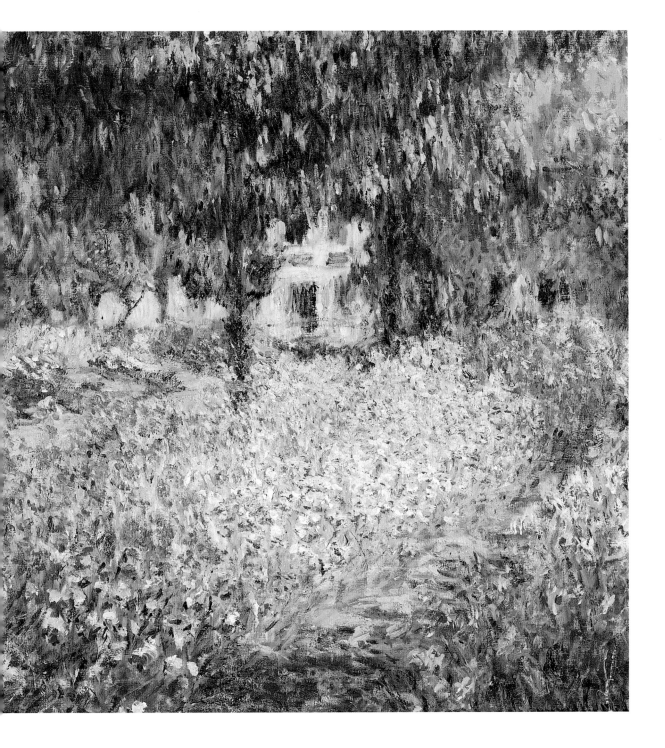

' ... it's not a meadow but a **virgin forest of flowers** whose colours are very pure, neither pink nor bluish but red or blue. '

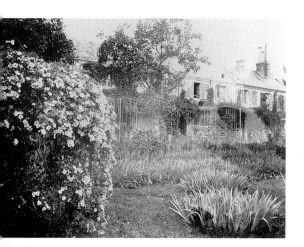

Above Massed flowers of *Clematis montana* are trained over an ironwork frame, shown on the left. Other climbers appear in the background, well established on the veranda.

Right Swathes of wild poppies filled the cornfields and meadows surrounding the village of Giverny. Monet selected their large herbaceous cousin, *Papaver orientale*, to bring a strong vibrant red into his garden.

by topping them with climbing roses. In time the spruce trees rotted, although he did not remove them until after he had put up the metal arches now familiar to visitors, in 1920, almost a decade after Alice's death.

The Grande Allée led from the main door to a gateway onto a public highway, the Chemin du Roi. With this exit, after 1895, were aligned the water garden's Japanese Bridge and a copper beech. The wide gravel path of the *allée* was lined with flower beds of the kind known as carp's back, in which the soil is built up centrally. Here it was ridged along the base of the spruces; later the double iron arches straddled the path from 'backbone' to 'backbone'. Climbing roses flower against a background of sky, whilst seasonal flowers in the beds on either side form a cascade to nasturtiums trailing across the gravel, gradually narrowing the path.

A pictorial composition

There are no statues, sculptures nor temples at Giverny. Excluding the greenhouses, the only garden structures apart from the bridges were the veranda *treillage* and various metal frameworks painted in Monet's chosen green. These had an important part to play in the overall composition. The creamy-yellow rose 'Mermaid' climbed up the veranda to bloom under Monet's bedroom window, and in summer a Virginia creeper provided dappled shade. In addition to the

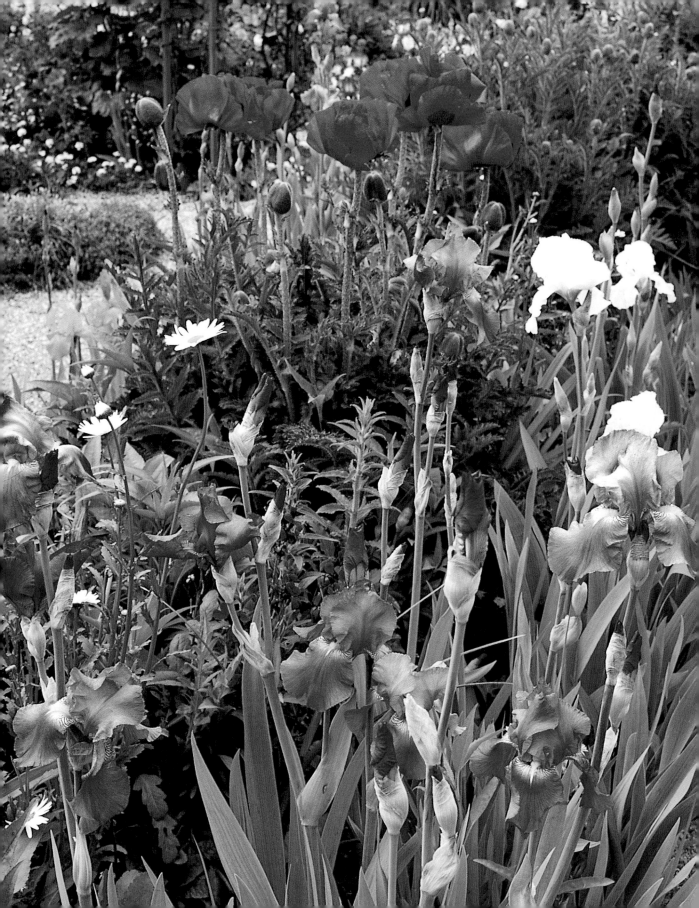

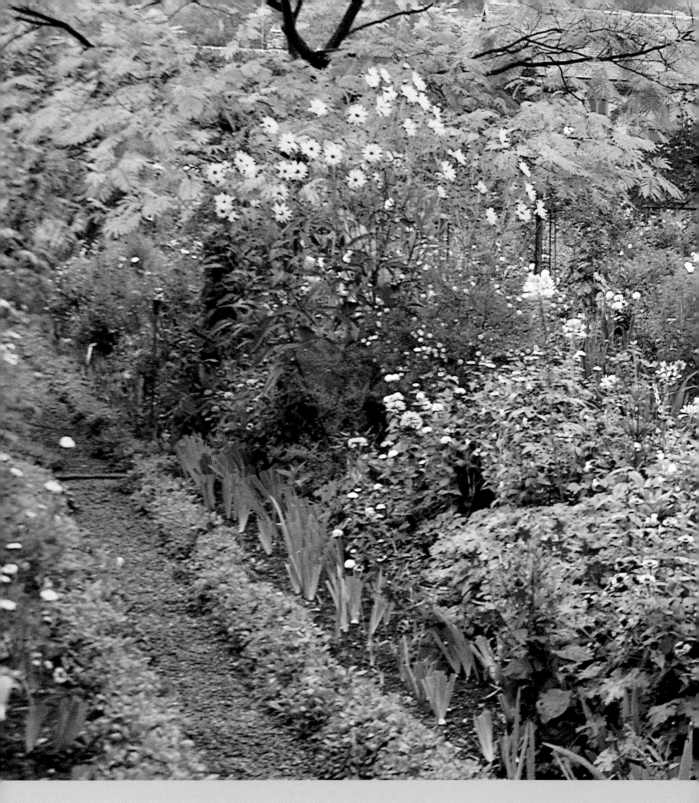

' ... all is obtained by a thousand tiny torches,

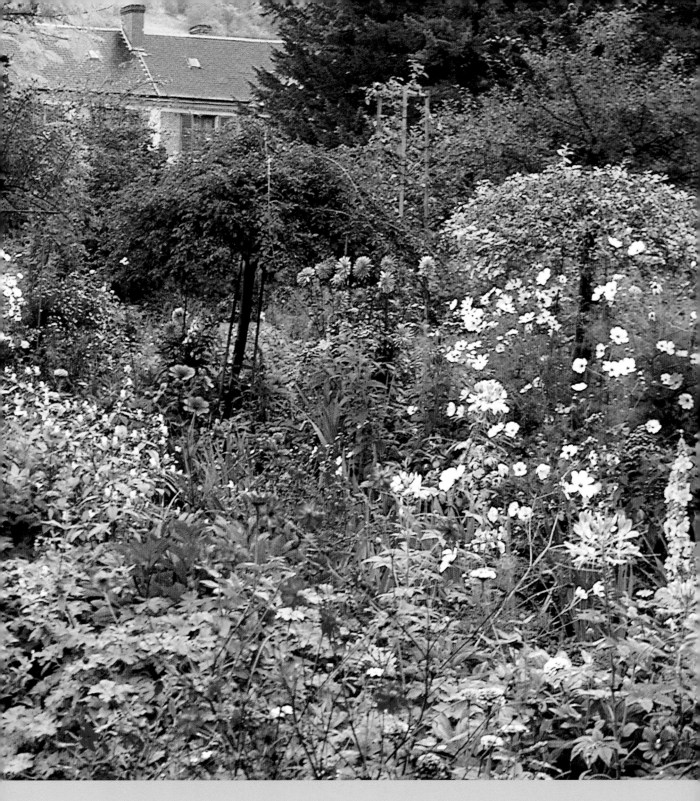

dancing in every direction like notes of colour.'

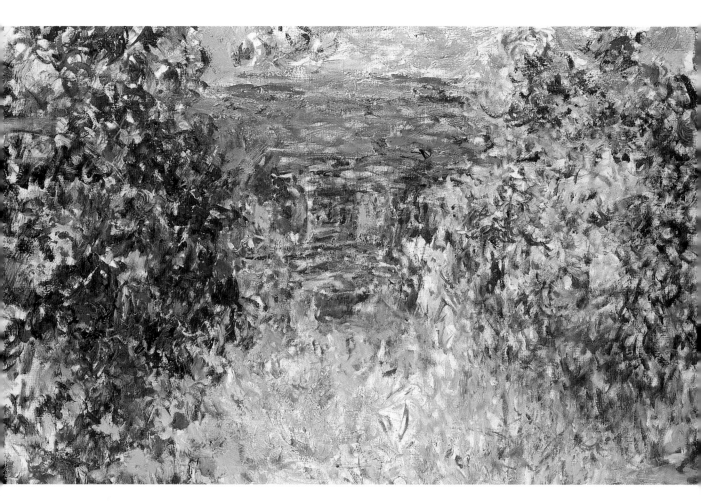

Previous page Afternoon sun highlights golden tints in the leaves of the immensely tall *Helianthus*, set against the delicate *Albizia julibrissin* (*left*) and the common mullein (*right*). Clumps of dahlias are broken by the showy heads of pink Cleomes and Cosmos.

arches of the Grande Allée, tripods gave height and colour by supporting nasturtiums and sweet peas, and weeping standard roses reached majestic proportions – among them the variety 'Belle Vichyssoise', which exists only at Giverny. Ingenious 'rooms' were created by means of small ironwork pavilions whose 'roofs' comprised a drapery of white or pink *Clematis montana*. These were planted above alternate 'paintbox' beds, giving dappled shade to the annuals and biennials below. By the 1880s, when Monet started work on the garden at Giverny, the fashion for the new earlier and larger-flowering varieties of clematis had been furthered since the introduction into Europe in the mid-19th century of Japanese clematis

Above Metal frameworks painted *le vert Monet* played an important part in the overall garden composition. On the left the rose supports can just be discerned in **The House seen from the Rose Garden**, *1922–4*, gently controlling the cascading roses so that they softly frame the house.

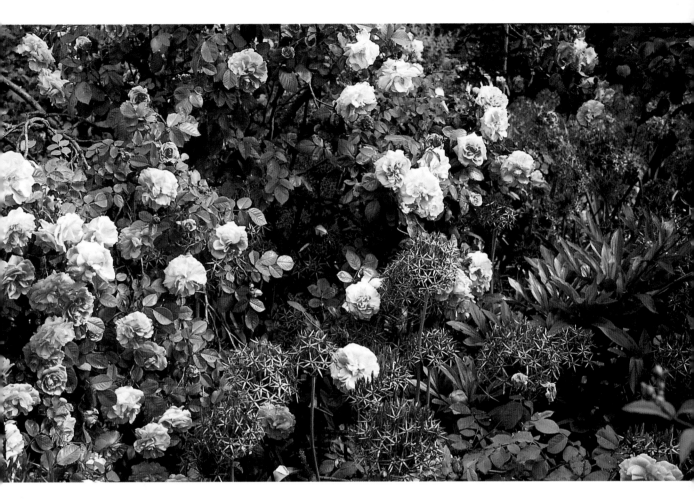

cultivars, which nurserymen had rapidly crossed with European and Chinese varieties.

The garden's rectangular beds slope from north to south and feature mass plantings of tulips, then irises, emerging from underplantings of aubrieta and hardy geraniums. The 38 'paintbox' flowerbeds are laid out in pairs from the top to the bottom of the garden and are planted in imitation of the true colours on Monet's paint palette. Beds run parallel to the Grande Allée, their mix of climbers and herbaceous perennial and annual plants giving an impressionistic effect focused by spikes of colour and sentinel standard roses. Monet worked on this upper area for ten years before acquiring the site of the

Above Monet was said to grow roses in every shape, form or colour. The full pink blooms of the rose 'Centenaire de Lourdes' in this glorious display cascade around upright allium heads.

water garden. Nonetheless, his most celebrated paintings of areas of the upper garden, such as *Irises, Giverny from the Rose Garden* and the series of views of the Grande Allée, were all undertaken some time later.

Gustave Caillebotte and fellow gardeners

One of the first visitors to the potager and apple orchards of the Maison du Pressoir was Gustave Caillebotte, who stayed for three days in June 1883. A fellow painter, he too was an

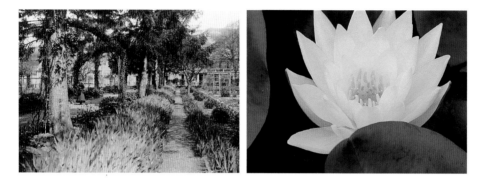

Above The stout trunks and branches of the spruces dominate the Grand Allée (*left*). The garden's first 'clematis rooms', in the top right, were constructed of small iron pavilions roofed with clematis. They were underplanted with colourful annual and herbaceous plants.

Above right Nymphaea Marliacea 'Chromatella', a brilliant hardy yellow water lily. Latour-Marliac hybridized European and American lilies to produce this for the Exposition Universelle, held in Paris in 1889.

enthusiastic gardener, with whom Monet freely exchanged plants and ideas. His own subsequent house and garden, bought ten years later, feature in the background of two of Monet's paintings of around 1872 – *Argenteuil, Boats Along the Riverbank* and *Boats Moored at Petit Gennevilliers*. At his family home some time before 1879, Caillebotte had painted *Yerres, on the Pond, Water Lilies*. Although only the yellow pond lily and white water lily were currently available, his use of reflection and absence of horizon predate Monet's work by nearly 30 years. Caillebotte's garden was arranged in a style similar to that of the upper garden at Giverny, featuring tall standard rose bushes and massed plantings of irises.

Over the years he and Monet sought out, bought and exchanged varieties of plants including chrysanthemums, lilacs, peonies, daisies, penstemons, hyacinths, sunflowers and poppies. Godefroy, a nurseryman based in Argenteuil, became

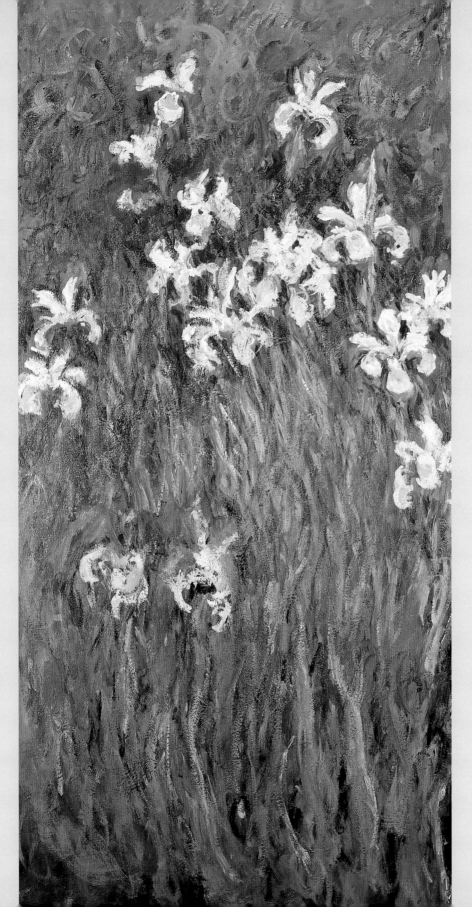

Left The dynamic
vertical emphasis of
Yellow Irises, *1914–7*,
provides a touch of
bright colour and
vivacity in the dark days
of World War I.

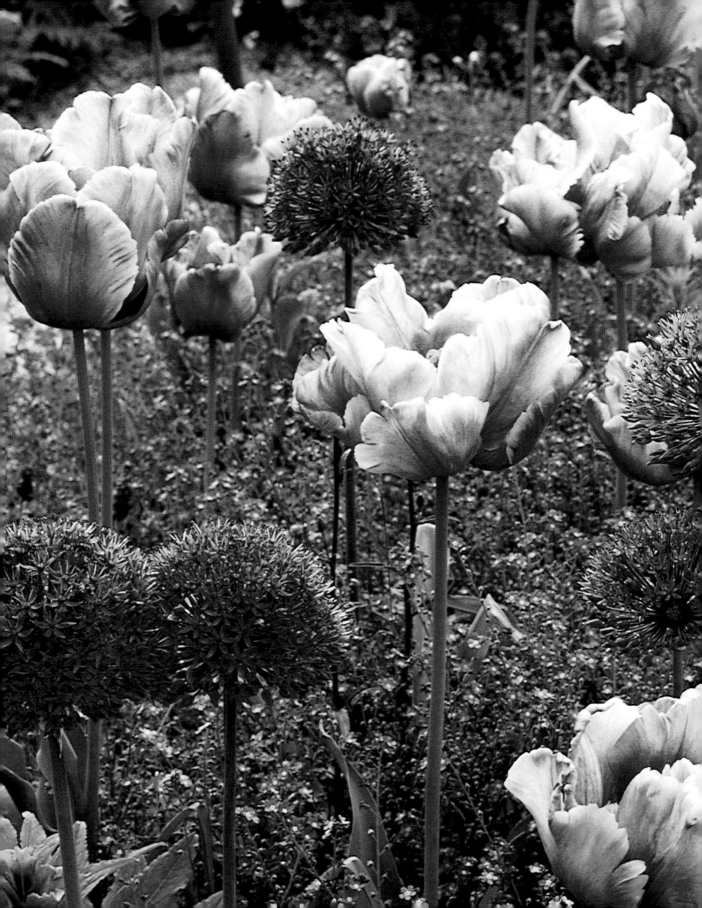

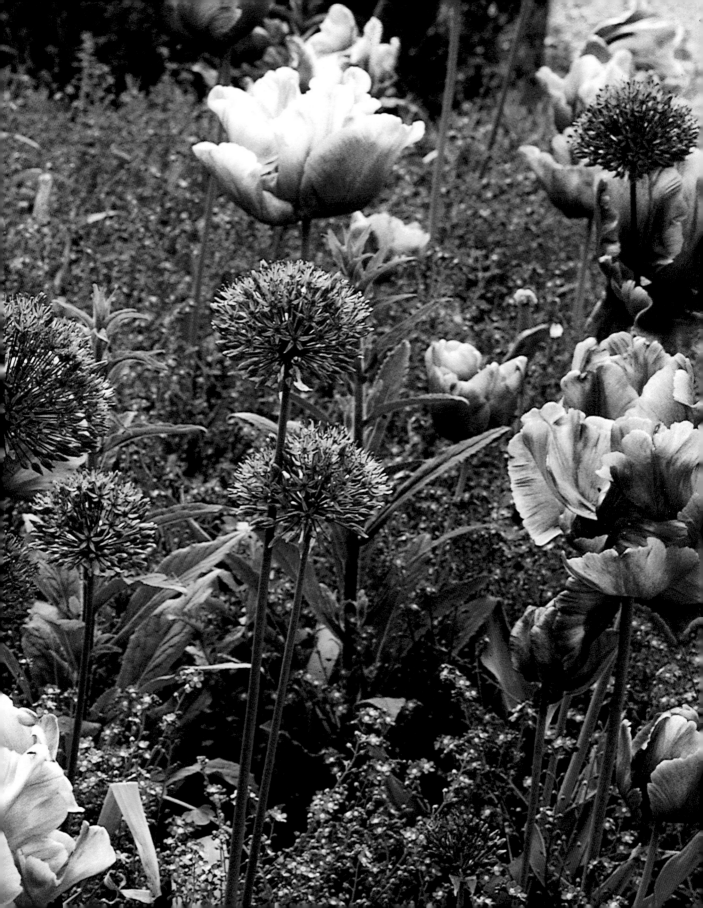

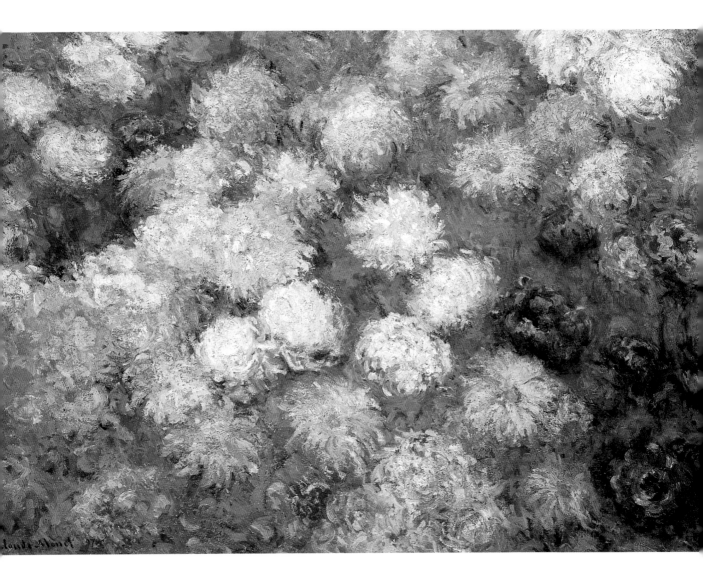

a good friend of Caillebotte and acquired many unusual plants both for him and for Monet. Meanwhile, Monet despatched dahlias to his friend and took in return all the fox-glove seeds Caillebotte could spare. Other similarities in taste can be glimpsed. As Monet gradually replaced the apple trees at Giverny with Japanese cherries and apricots, the rough grass beneath became lawns interspersed with 'baskets' of flowers. Caillebotte's spring painting of his garden at Petit

Previous page A harmony in blue, alliums echo the dark striations of the tulips, both standing proud from a sea of forget-me-nots.

'His life is what he paints; and what he paints is his life … He wants only one thing, to immerse himself in colour … He adores the whole beauty of nature, which he sees around him and which tortures him, for that is what he is so anxious to translate into paint – the innumerable, ever-changing beauties of nature.'

Gennevilliers likewise shows a flowering cherry and a 'basket' of pansies. Rather than a formal bouquet of blooms, these flowers were meant to look as though they had been gathered from the wild. Both gardens included almost identical greenhouses, Monet's being influenced by Caillebotte's, and their owners shared a passion for tender orchids.

Photographs of Giverny capture the garden's role as a host in its own right to family and friends, in an atmosphere of easy

Above left Monet painted chrysanthemums indoors and out, relishing the petals' texture and harmonious colours. **Chrysanthemums**, *1897*, is one of four paintings portraying large, jostling blooms that seem to float on the canvas.

'I DO WHAT
I CAN TO
EXPRESS
WHAT I FEEL
IN THE
PRESENCE
OF NATURE.'

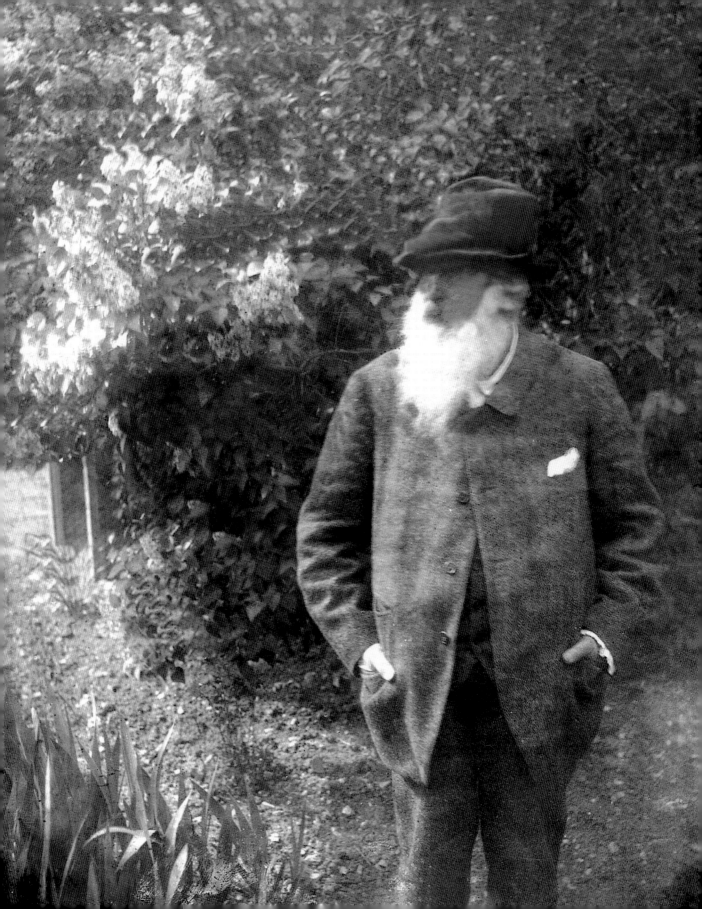

enjoyment that is echoed by the picture *Women in the Garden*. The subtleties of its layout and the splendour of its planting gave joy to many, and Monet expressed his own pleasure by despatching plants and produce to friends all over France. As well as Caillebotte, his dearest friends Clemenceau, Geffroy and Mirbeau all shared his passion for gardening; Clemenceau received from him great quantities of anthemis and gladioli for his garden at Bel Ebat in La Vendée. Mme Pissarro gardened with not a sou to spend, so imagine her delight, having admired the irises at Giverny, when she found that Monet had despatched a generous collection to her by train. The Renoirs and the Monets were regular visitors to each others' home, and as a keen gardener, Aline Renoir was another enthusiast who swapped plants with Monet.

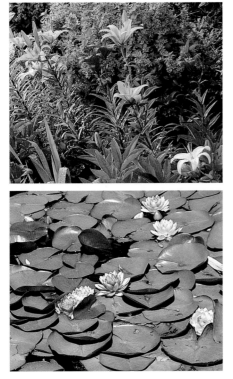

The Water Garden

Screened by high walls around the gardens of the Maison du Pressoir, the adjacent Chemin du Roi was both a road and a railway. Monet partly removed the wall and replaced it with ironwork through which he trained *Tropaeolum speciosum*. In this way passing travellers could also enjoy his gardens; when the advent of cars brought clouds of dust, he paid to have the road tarred. In 1893 he bought a piece of meadow beyond the road and railway with plans to make a water garden. However, this project raised opposition from residents and the municipal council. Local people were aware of Monet's botanic enthusiasm and had become convinced that the 'foreign' plants he intended to grow were potential health hazards. An indignant letter from

Left (*top*) Japanese and Chinese lilies, in yellows, pinks and reds as well as white, transformed Monet's flowerbeds. In an attractive fusion of east and west, they here offset the invasive North American Goldenrod.

Left (*bottom*) Rather than use the official name for the water lily, *Nymphaea*, Monet referred to them as '*Nymphéas*' – pink-petticoated nymphs gently dancing in their surrounding leaves.

Right Monet rose regularly at 5.30 am to study the sky from his bedroom window. Often he was by the pool in time for sunrise in order to record the early morning shafts of sunlight contrasting with the curtains of willow and drapes of wisteria.

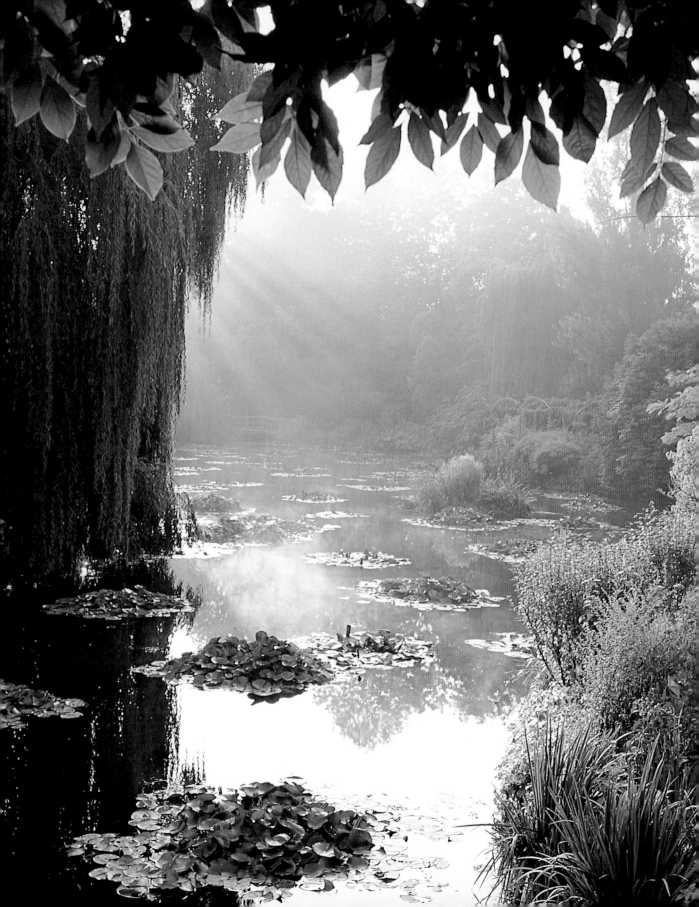

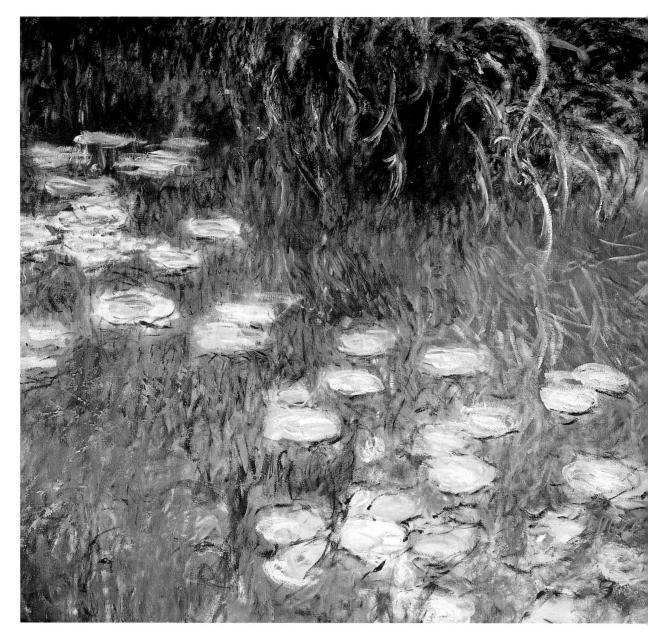

Above A detail from **Water Lilies**: **Morning**, *c.1925*, captures the potent atmosphere of the breaking day. A rising sun throws white light across the leaves and flowers of a willow, casting flickering reflections across the water.

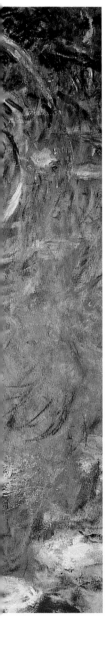

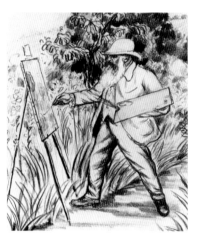

'I'm slaving away, working determinedly at a series of effects, but at this time of year the sun goes down so fast I can't keep up with it.'

Monet to the Préfet du Eure on 17 July defends his plans 'to supply a pond where I would like to grow aquatic plants ... it is merely intended for leisure and to delight the eye and also to provide motifs to paint ... I will grow plants such as water lilies, reeds, different varieties of irises ... no question of poisoning the water'.

The work was largely undertaken in the latter half of 1893, interspersed with requests to Durand-Ruel for advances to help fund it. The excavation of the pond had been completed by January of the following year, and the Japanese Bridge was erected at much the same time. Monet made his first painting of it before leaving for a visit to Norway, from where he worried about the consequences of the pond freezing over during a bitterly cold French winter. A number of inspired and innovative plantsmen were instrumental in helping Monet realize his plans. One was Joseph Bory Latour-Marliac, who succeeded in hybridizing water lilies and introduced European gardeners to a panoply of Chinese and Japanese bamboos and water plants. An incidental factor in his achievements, in particular the successful cultivation of water lilies, was that his nursery at Temple sur Lot, in the southwest of France, enjoyed some of the world's highest light values. Latour-

Above Monet in action among the flowers, as recorded in this sketch by Manzana Pissarro. The easel seems to rear out of the ground while Monet, palette in hand and surrounded by his flowers, captures the instant on his canvas.

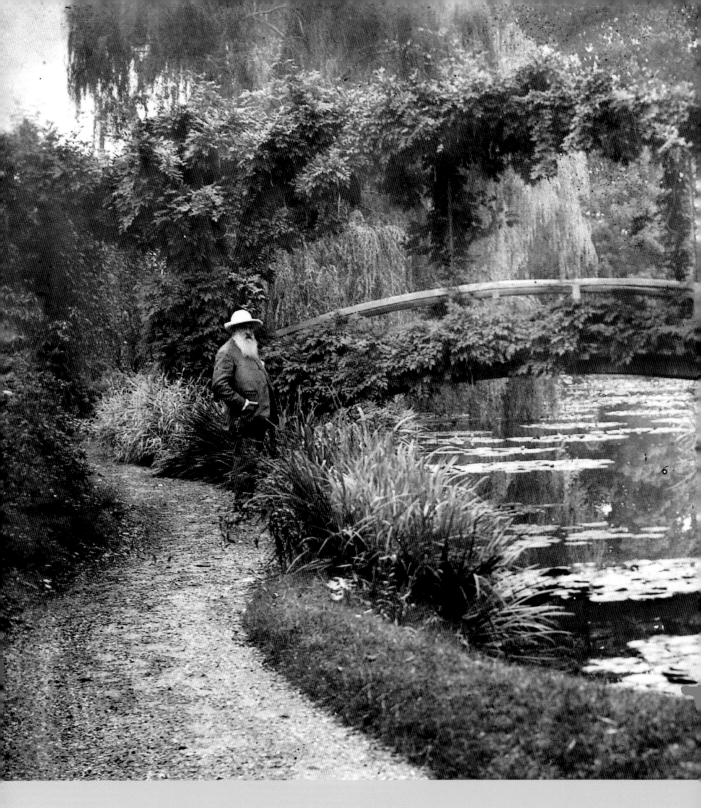

'Leaving Giverny would upset me greatly ...

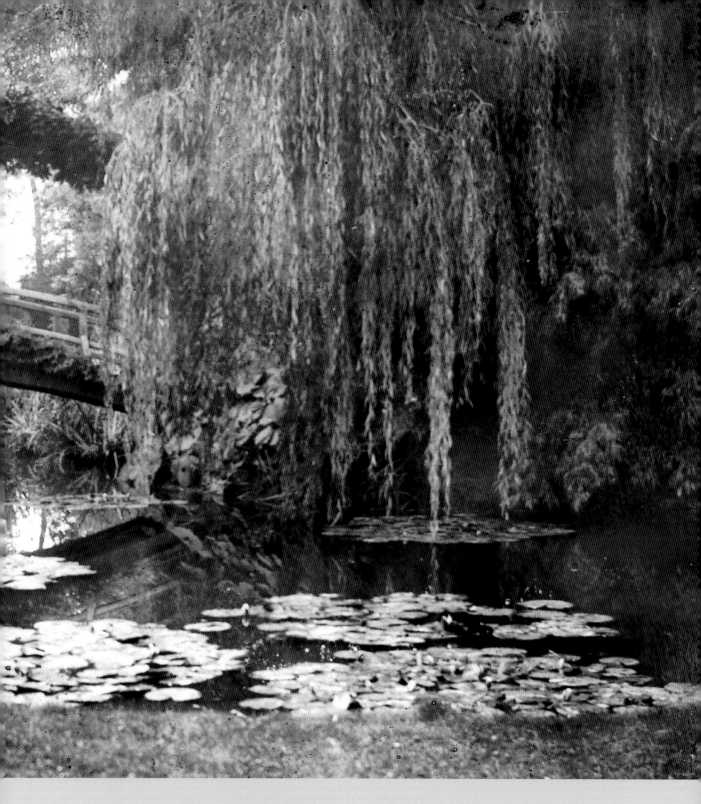

I would never find such a beautiful place.'

Marliac kept meticulous copies of every letter, order and article, bound in volumes, from 1881 to his death in 1911, a practice continued by his family until 1924. His correspondence
and magazine articles of 1888 and 1889 detail the results of a
decade's work hybridizing water lilies, which culminated in his
award of first prize at the 1889 Exposition Universelle. Here,
Paris itself was on display, its art and its industry set forth
among spectacular show gardens. Latour-Marliac's 1889
booklet *Les Aquariums de plein air, de serre et d'apparement* anticipated Monet's interest in its account of growing water lilies:
'... so this picture full of seduction has provoked massive
enthusiasm amongst the happy owners of lakes, fishponds,
streams and pools ...'. It was a burgeoning gardening trend
that Monet was to adapt to suit his own purposes. William
Robinson dedicated the 1893 44th volume of *The Garden* to
Latour-Marliac, 'who has brought the colours and forms of

Below Monet's lily pond
in the 1930s fulfils the
original conception of
1893 in an intricate
composition of lilies,
reeds and irises.
Textures and colours
complement and con-
trast in a serene and
harmonious pattern.

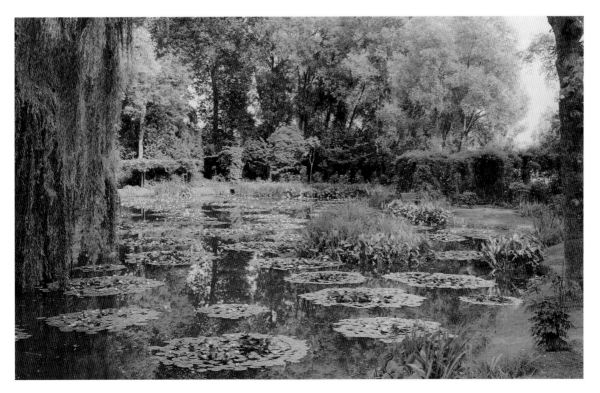

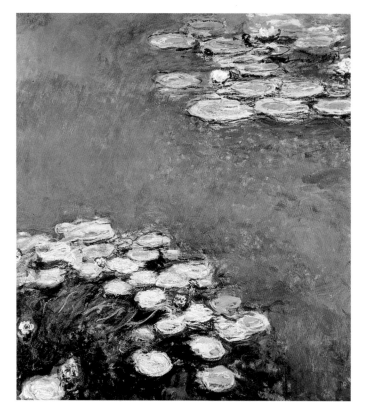

Left The dominant green hues of reflected willow trees contrast with the areas of blue sky and sunlight in ***Water Lilies***, *c.1914–7*. A cool green channel divides the two plant groups, complementing the dense texture of the glaucous leaves.

the water lilies of the east to the waters of the north.'

Monet's purchases from this source included several rare species of decorative water plants: in 1894, for example, he put in a large order for water lilies and other, in some cases unusual, water and bog plants. In the following April he acquired ten hydropyrum; in May 1896 he ordered specimens of the exotic water lilies *Nymphaea zanzibarensis azurea* and *Nymphaea stellata* at ten francs each. Sadly, though, the exotic area of his water garden was a failure.

As elsewhere, however, work on this part of the garden and its design was continuous. In 1901, Monet extended the length of the water garden from 20 to 60 metres (65-200 ft), and then two years later he added an upper gallery to the bridge. He planted and trained purple wisteria over its lower rails and strong-scented white wisteria over the new upper section of the bridge. In 1904 he purchased from Latour-Marliac four rare varieties of water lily costing 20 francs and 25 francs

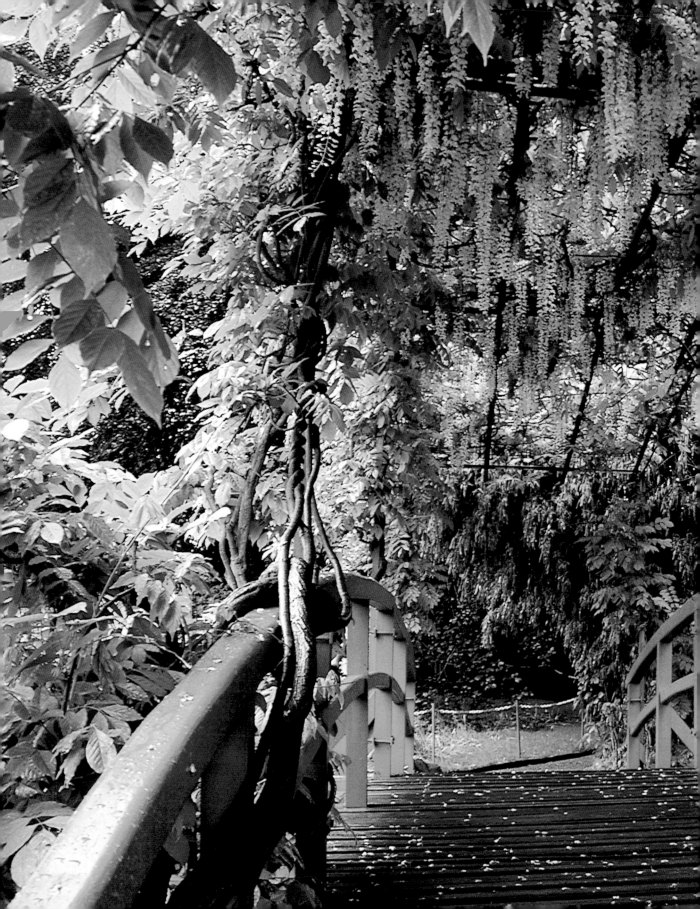

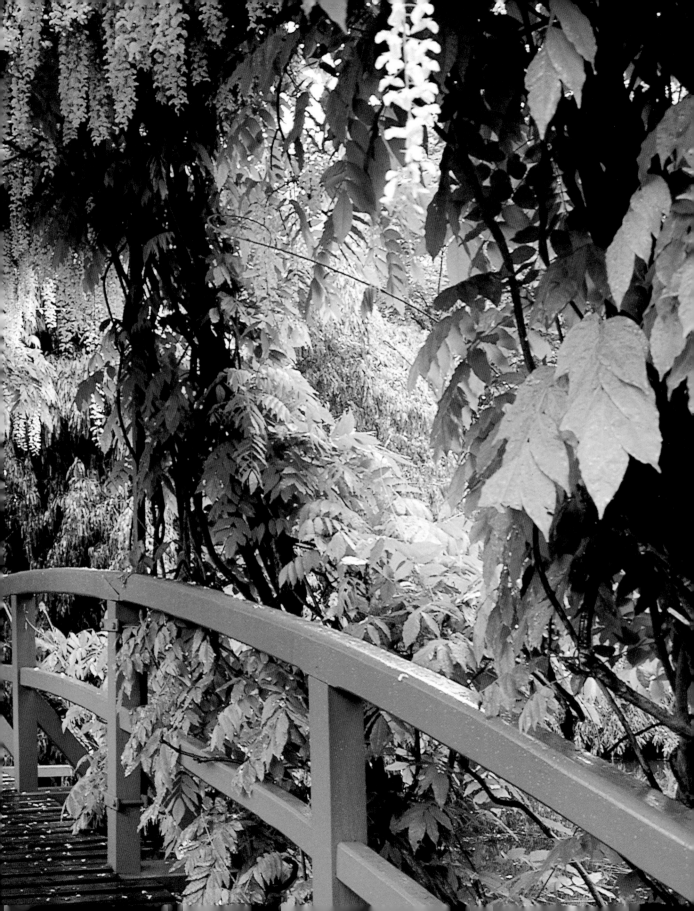

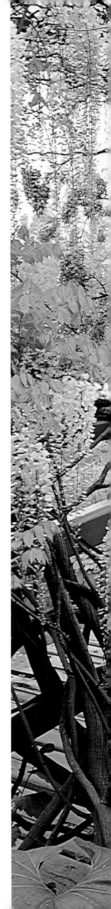

Previous page When in flower the wisteria on the Japanese Bridge assails you with intense scent. The leaves, with their heavy pendant flowers, create a dense ceiling to the bridge's 'room with a view'.

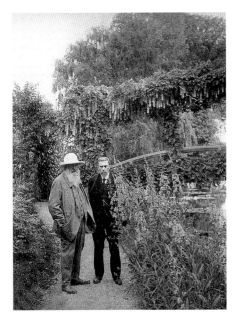

Left Monet with a close friend, the journalist and critic Gustave Geffroy. A great admirer of Monet's work, Geffroy wrote that Shakespeare's poetry had taken a subtle possession of the water garden.

Right Monet chose to paint the Japanese Bridge green rather than the customary vermilion. In this way, its curving horizontal lines could blend with the wisteria and surrounding lush greenery as an almost organic structure.

each: the hardy hybrids 'Arethusa', 'Atropurpurea', 'William Falconer' and 'James Brydon'. By 1905, the pool's now familiar covering of lily pads had materialized, increasing the seemingly immaterial quality of the water's surface. A vertical emphasis was given along the margins of the pond by the weeping willows, whose trailing leaves and branches took the eye irresistibly back into the limpid water below. Within the

'Everything looks wonderful at the moment and the light is dazzling.'

nearby bamboo thicket, Monet carved out a semi-circular shape to provide a sheltered viewpoint overlooking the water.

Apparently, in the early years of the century the nursery at Temple sur Lot was visited by Monet in person. This was the result of a rather more expensive purchase, in October 1904, of a new car, in which he and Alice drove to Spain.

Another influential nurseryman from whom over the years Monet bought many plants was Georges Truffaut, editor of

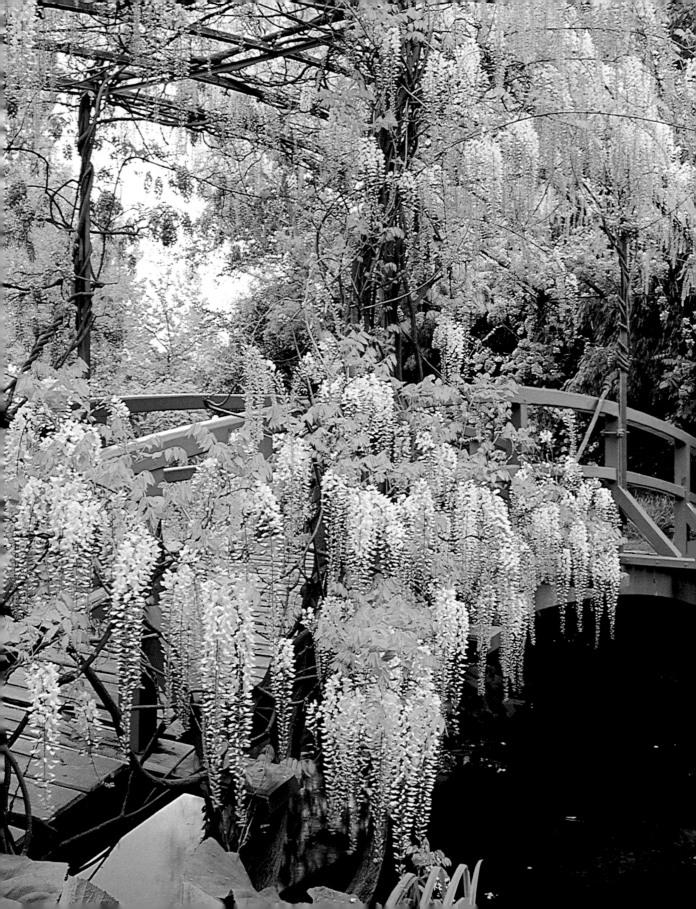

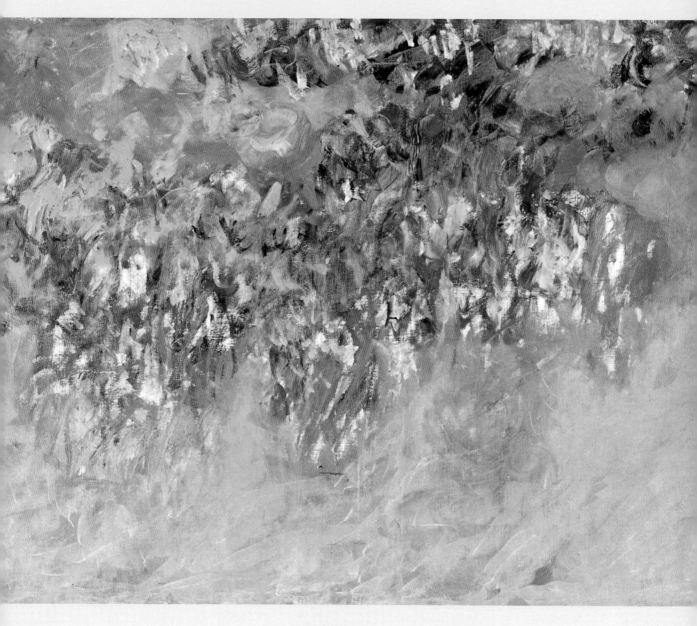

Above Wisteria in the water garden was supported on a framework at the pond's edge. In the ambiguous perspective of ***Wisteria**, 1919–20*, the flowers may be cascading against a blue sky or reflected in water amidst the pink clouds of a summer's day.

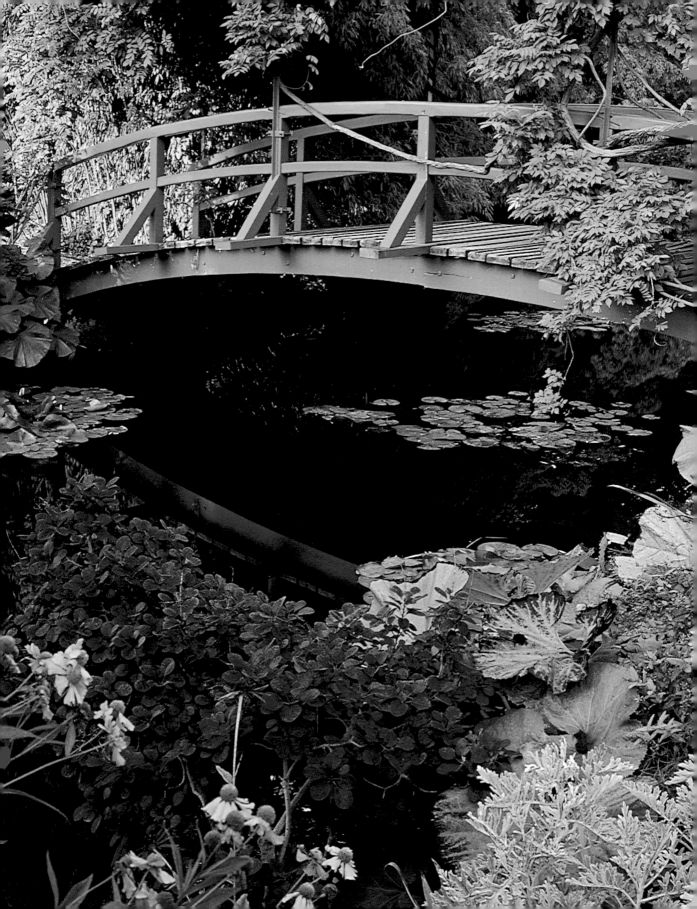

the magazine *Jardinage*. In October 1913, he published an article on irises for water gardens, written by Monet's head gardener, Félix Breuil; a piece by Truffaut himself about Monet's garden appeared in November 1924. Monet also bought many varieties originally bred by Pierre Louis Victor Lemoine, who had introduced nearly a hundred new species into cultivation and had hybridized a number of tropical and sub-tropical plants, hardy herbaceous perennials, as well as trees and shrubs, including lilac and philadelphus.

Oriental influences

Monet firmly denied that, unlike many so-called 'Japanese' gardens recently created in France, England and the United States, his own plans had been influenced by oriental traditions. Despite such protestations, his sensitive response to nature had much in common with the origins of Japanese garden design. This had evolved from a combination of practical agrarian traditions, the spiritual responses of Shinto to the selection of a natural object and its surroundings as a sacred place, and Buddhism, which introduced the Chinese tradition of 'lake and island' designs. Monet tended towards spiritual values close to those of Zen Buddhism – enlightenment through meditation, reflection and 'sudden understanding'.

Certainly in Monet's water garden the qualities of *wabi* (rustic solitude) and *yungen* (tranquillity) were successfully evoked. The bridge, added in 1895, approximates to a Japanese style, albeit painted in Monet's green rather than vermilion, but in general the paraphernalia of tea-houses and lanterns was alien to Monet. Alone or with family and guests, he strolled in his garden more or less as a ritual, engrossed in the sinuous outline where earth and water meet, the play of light on the pool, and reflections cast from the water's surface. Guests arriving in the late afternoon were hastened to see the water lilies before their flowers closed up at evening's approach.

Left A late summer sun at around midday illuminates the bamboo over the bridge with a rich glow. It contrasts with the deep blue hydrangea blooms and the delicate silver cineraria in the foreground.

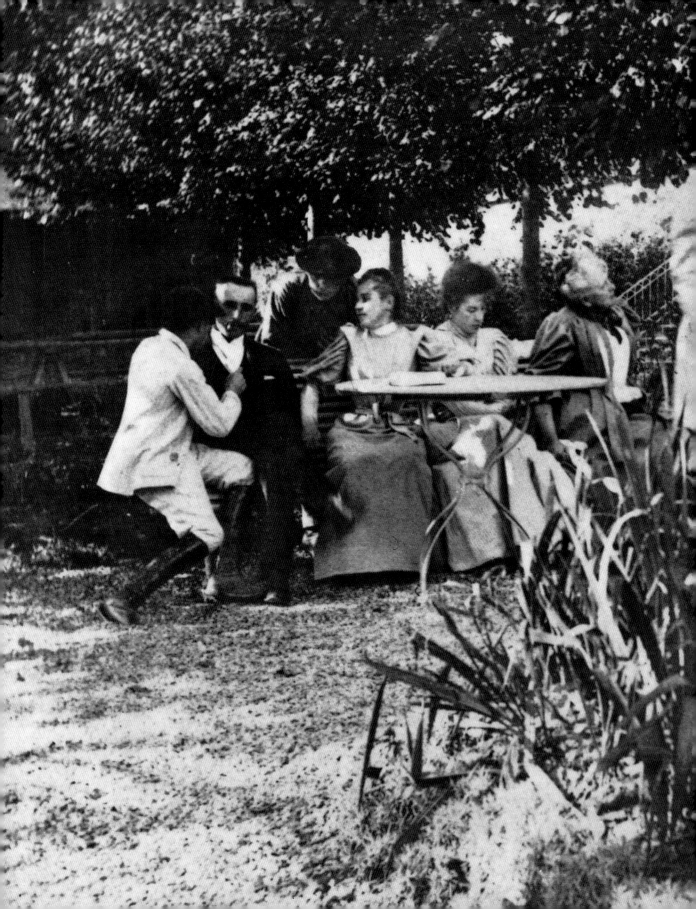

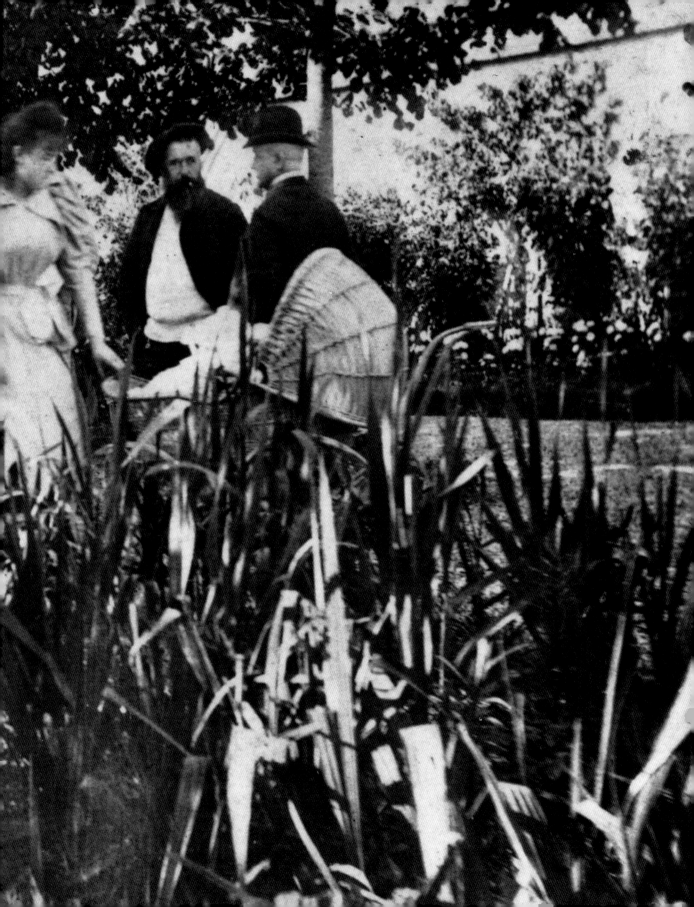

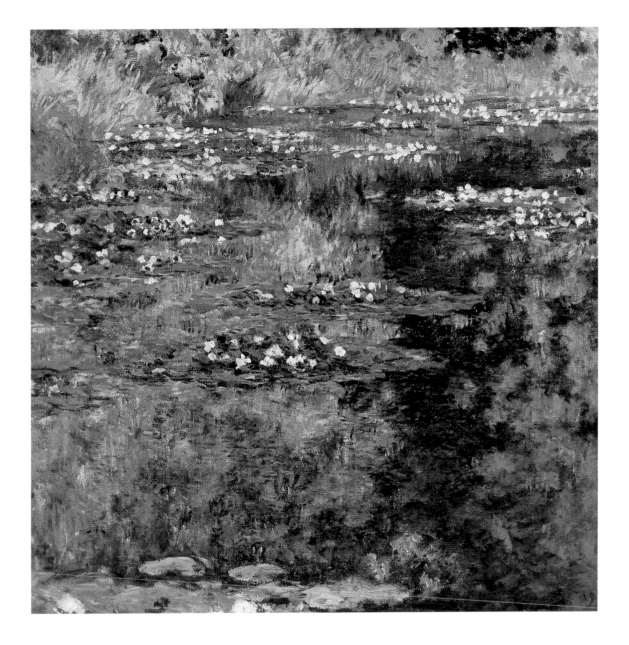

'I'm extremely busy with my garden; it's such a joy

A number of oriental plants were brought to Giverny directly from the Far East, by visitors such as the Japanese Princess Matsukata and her husband, who presented a gift of tree peonies and lilies. Many species favoured by Monet featured in Japanese prints of the time, including wisteria, chrysanthemum, peony, cherry, water lily, iris and bamboo. In Japanese gardens bamboo was valued not just for its beauty but for its practicality and its ability to bend rather than break. One of the first nurserymen to introduce it into Europe was Latour-Marliac, whose records for 1883 show 23 varieties arriving at Temple sur Lot from Japan, 17 of which survived, followed by a further 19 varieties the next year.

The three gardens

By 1889 Monet had enjoyed three years of high earnings: in 1886, 25,000 francs; in 1887, 44,000 francs; and 28,000 francs in 1888. As his financial circumstances improved, so did the number of gardeners in his hire. The first started in 1891, and eventually the number rose to seven, including one man employed to ensure each day that the appearance of the lily pool remained immaculate. In 1897 the former head gardener was succeeded, on the recommendation of Mirbeau, by Félix Breuil, whose father worked in the same capacity for Mirbeau senior. Breuil was replaced after World War I by

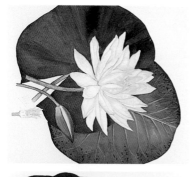

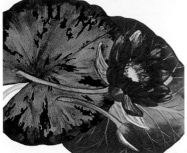

Above Botanical watercolour illustrations in horticultural journals and catalogues record the individual characteristics of plants. Monet subscribed to several such publications to keep up with new varieties. Those shown here are *Nymphaea odorata* 'Sulphurea Grandiflora' by Alix *(above)* and *Nymphaea* 'William Falconer' by JP *(below)*.

to me and ... I am in raptures at the wonders of nature.'

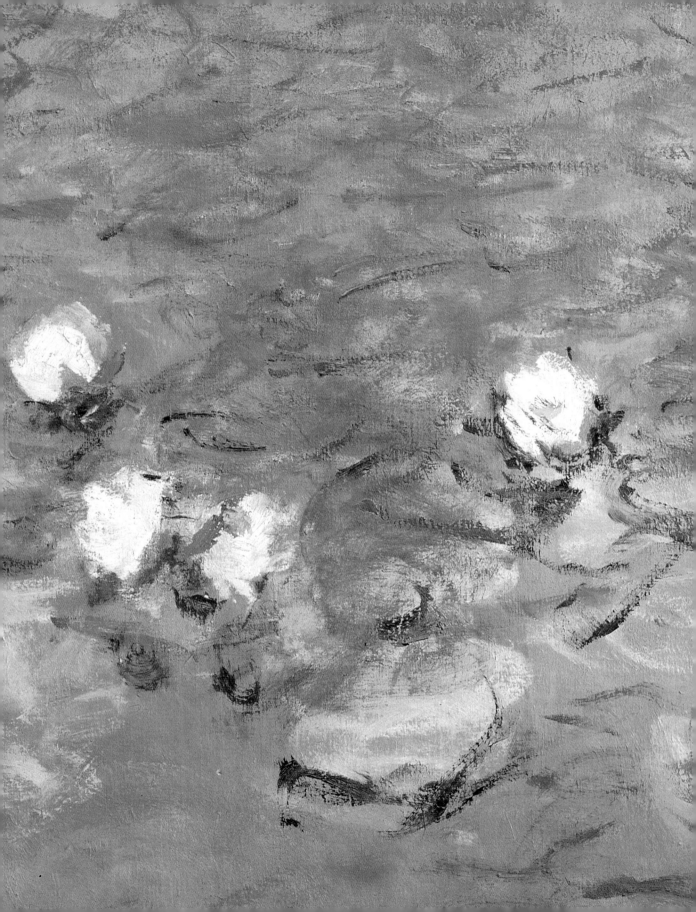

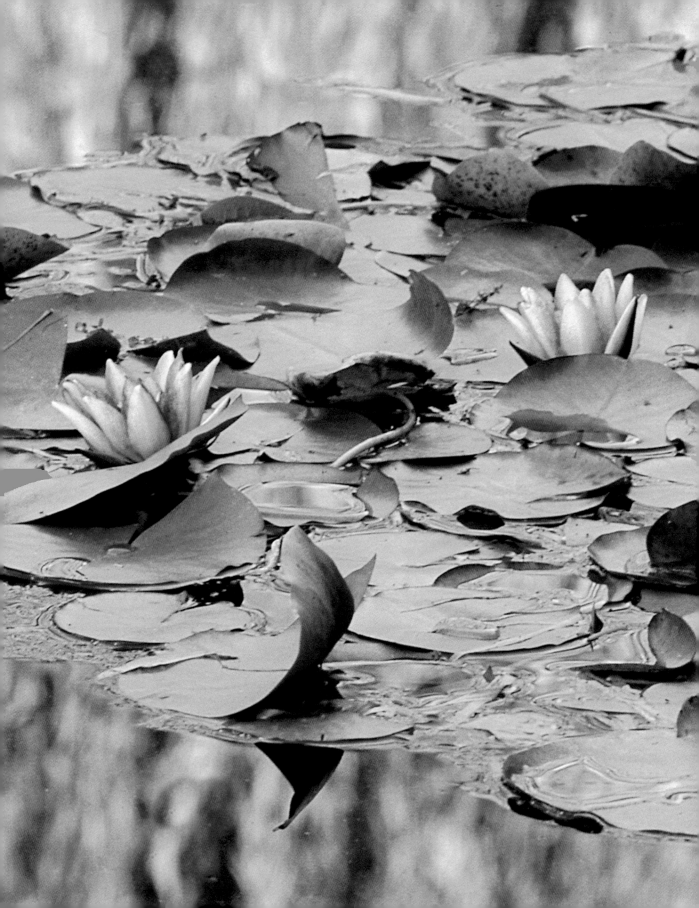

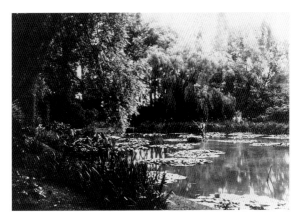

Above A gardener on the *norvégienne* boat checks the placement of the pool's lilies and cleans the surface of the water. One gardener was employed full-time to maintain the lily pond

Léon Lebret, who maintained the garden in splendid condition during Monet's lifetime; under the watchful eye of Blanche, he continued as head gardener until his death during World War II.

Monet was meticulous in orchestrating the garden's maintenance. Notes have survived, probably written in February 1900 before Monet's departure on a visit to London, which give comprehensive instructions. The notes about sowing instruct around 300 pots of poppies, 60 of sweet peas, 60 of white agrimony, and 30 of yellow agrimony. Blue salvia, blue water lilies in beds (in the greenhouse), dahlias and *Iris kaempferi* were also to be sown. The detailed notes continue with the following instructions: 'From 15th-25th, lay the dahlias down to root; plant out those with shoots before I get back (early April). Don't forget the lily bulbs. Should the Japanese peonies arrive plant them immediately if weather permits, taking care initially to protect buds from the cold, as much as from the heat of the sun. Get down to pruning: rose trees not too long, except for the thorny varieties. In March sow the grass seeds, plant out the little nasturtiums, keep a close eye on the gloxinia, orchids, etc., in the

Previous page In this detail of **Water Lilies**: **Morning**, *c.1925* (*left*), one of the *Grandes Décorations* canvases, the bright leaves and flowers appear to be in gentle movement on the surface of the pond. The photograph (*right*) captures the instant of light and *sensation* in an artistic compostion.

Right In another of Monet's 'Water Lily' works, the effects of sun and sky pour across the surface of his pool. The plants in **Water Lilies**, *1907*, seem almost scorched by the reflected fiery colours.

' ... the further I get the more I realize how much I have to work in order **to capture what I am looking for: "instantaneity",** above all, the same enveloping light spread over everything.'

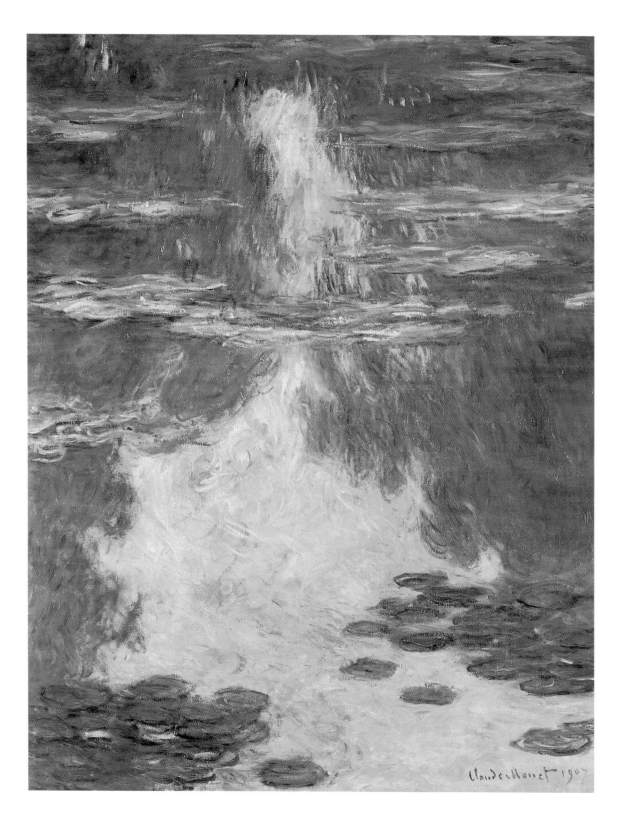

greenhouse, as well as the plants under frames. Trim the borders as arranged: put wires in for the clematis and climbing roses as soon as Picard has done the necessary. If the weather's bad, make some straw matting, but lighter than previously. Plant cuttings from the rose trees at the pond around manure in the hen huts. Don't delay work on tarring the planks and plant the *Helianthus latiflorus* in good clumps right away. If anything's missing such as manure, pots etc., ask Madame if possible on a Friday so as to have it on Saturday. In March force the chrysanthemums along as the buds won't open in damp conditions; and don't forget to put the sulphur sheets back over the greenhouse frames.'

Following his purchase of the Maison Bleue, Monet installed M Florimond to take charge of food production, and in the walled garden fruits, vegetables, mushrooms, herbs and spices were grown. Despite their variety, all three gardens at Giverny corresponded to their owner's tastes. There was the kaleidoscopic colour and gaiety of the area nearest the house; elsewhere was the serenity of the water garden, reflecting another aspect of Monet; and then there was the gourmand

'I am more and more enflamed by the need to

produce from the Maison Bleue, fit for a man who enjoyed his food. It meant much to Monet that in winter he and his guests could still enjoy flowers native to a more propitious clime.

His neighbour Lilla Cabot Perry recounted that one autumn when she and her husband arrived in Giverny there was great excitement over the Monets' new greenhouse. The new heating system had just been installed and Monet was so concerned lest it failed to work that he decided to spend the night in the greenhouse, which had already been filled with plants, in order to keep an eye on it. Nothing would dissuade

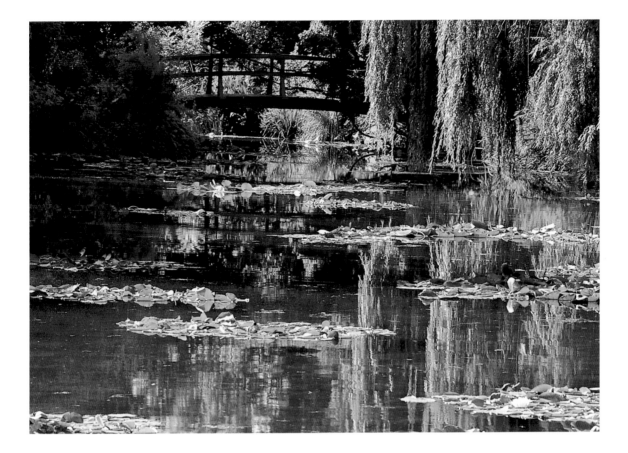

render accurately what I experience.'

him, so Alice prepared to join his vigil. This caused an outcry amongst the girls, who felt they would be failing in their duties if they were not there to care for their parents. So the entire household camped out with the gloxinias for the night – and the heating, inevitably, ran impeccably.

In descriptions of Monet's garden, much is made of the colours, set against earth, sky or water. A further element loved by him were the movements and sounds of birds and butterflies: the bright flash of kingfishers, swallows or red admirals. His garden included a large aviary that housed par-

Above Monet was fascinated by the *sensations* of light on unfurling buds and leaves, as well as by the daily opening and closing of individual flowers. Guests arriving in the late afternoon were rushed down to the pool to watch the water lilies close.

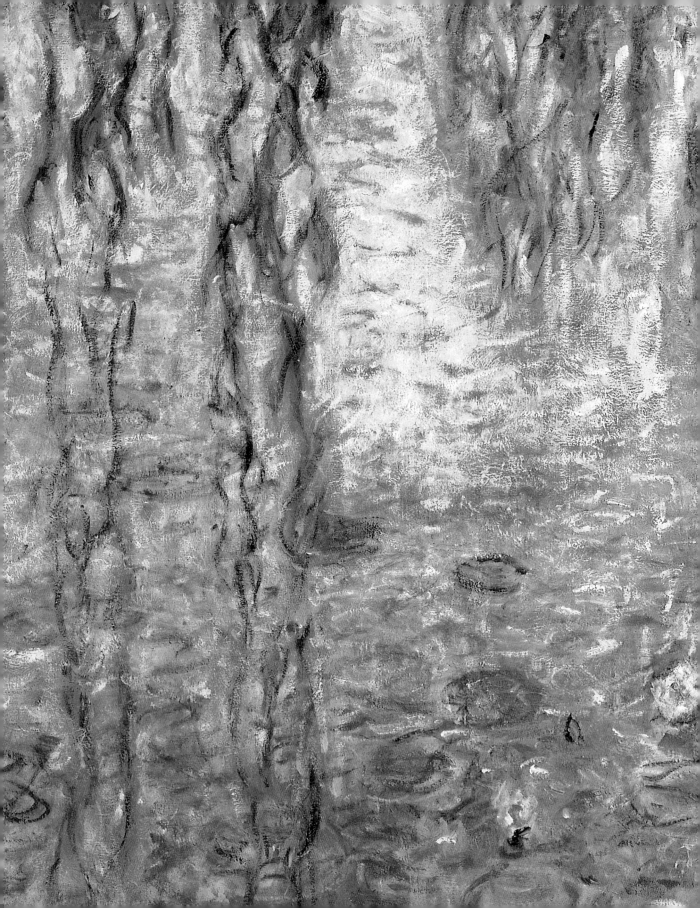

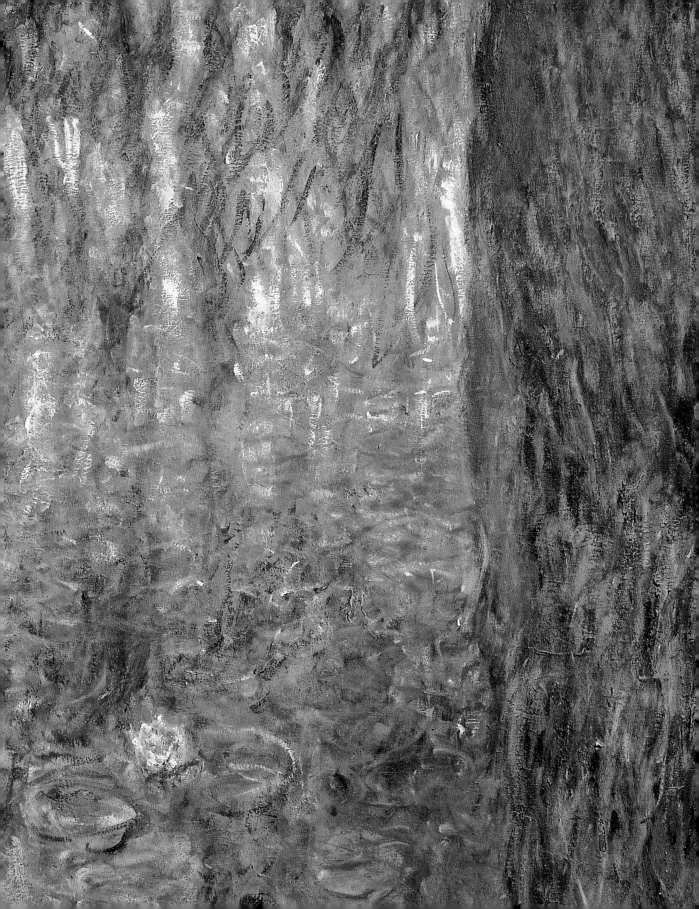

rots and grazing tortoises, and there were enclosures for peacocks, golden and common pheasants, black ducks and white hens. The hen run near the house became a nursing home for wounded birds, gulls and larks, and for over three years a one-legged sparrow took breadcrumbs from the table.

The dominant sounds in the garden included the hum of bees, the babbling of the tiny diverted River Ru, happy chat-

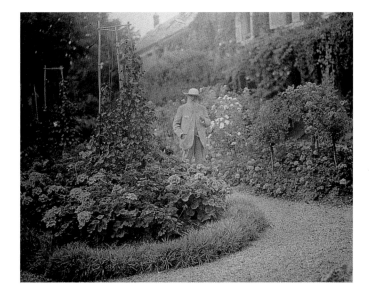

Left Monet stands among flower beds near his house, *c*.1923. A mass of pelargoniums is edged with clove scented pinks; central height is provided by red roses scrambling over a painted iron frame. Behind, the house seems to disappear under a rampant virginia creeper and the rose-swathed veranda.

Right The boundaries of land and water seem to merge in **The Water Lily Pond at Giverny**, *1917*. The green of the banks seems to melt into the water and the sun glows fiercely through willow branches, creating a slate-blue effect. Monet donated this painting to the Musée de Grenoble as an encouragement to other modern artists.

ter, the raucous call of peacocks, and other birdsong. Monet apparently said that he wanted 'to paint as a bird sings' – an assertion that irritated Jean-Pierre Hoschedé, however, who maintained that his stepfather had been misquoted, pointing out that unlike birdsong Monet's paintings were never an endlessly repeated refrain. Whatever the truth of this, in his garden Monet always welcomed the surrounding sound of birdsong and the sense of season that it brought.

Setbacks suffered at Giverny included severe flooding, which in the winter of 1909–10 caused damage across the whole region. Monet made two donations to the village; meanwhile the water garden, the Chemin du Roi and part of the upper garden had been inundated. On 10 February

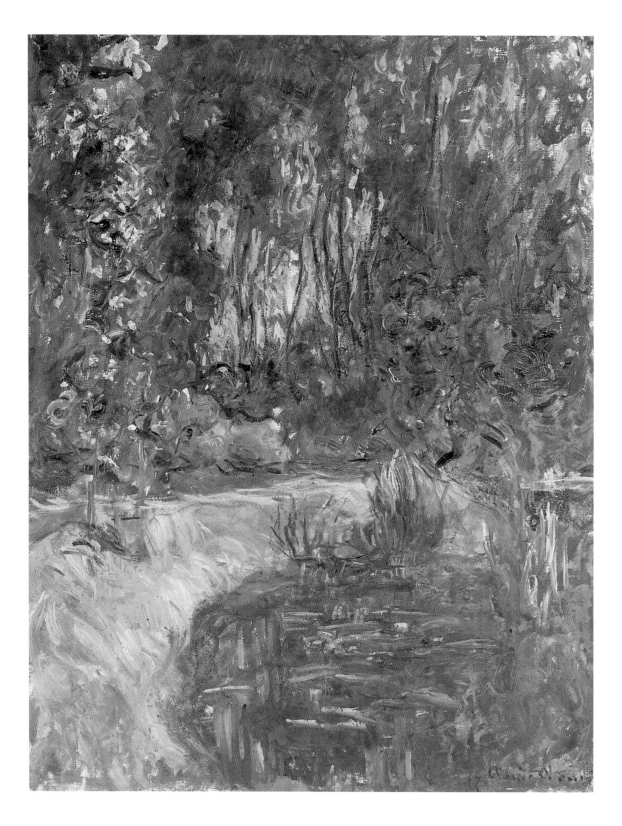

261

262

Monet wrote to Paul Durand Ruel: 'I thought for a while that my entire garden would be destroyed... although I've lost a lot of plants, it will probably be less calamitous than I feared.' On 5 August, however, he told Bernheim-Jeune that 'to add to my miseries an appalling storm has created havoc in my garden. The weeping willows I was so proud of have been torn apart and stripped; the finest entirely broken up. In short, a real disaster and a real worry for me.' In repairing the damage, Monet took the opportunity of making the pool more curvaceous than the original design and of generally extending the water garden.

The misery of Alice's death in 1911 left him absolutely bereft. Monet's artistic genius was established by the time he arrived at Giverny, but it was Alice who provided the catalyst for him to practise the ancient skill of landscaping by harmonizing nature as art and capturing, in the words of Alexander Pope, 'The Genius of the Place'. Her death was followed by that of Jean in 1914, intensifying Monet's bereavement; the onset of cataracts added to a burden that wors-

Left In 1894 the celebrated Latour-Marliac nurseries despatched a large order of water and bog plants to Giverny. The colours were diverse: *Nymphaea flava* and *sulfurea grandiflora* are yellow-flowering; *N. Laydeckeri 'Rosea'* is pink. *Nelumbium japonicum roseum* is lilac-pink; and *N. 'Osiris'* is deep carmine pink. *N. speciosum rosea* is the pink Egyptian lotus and *N. album* is the white lotus flower.

' ... the garden took up some of my time as I want to have

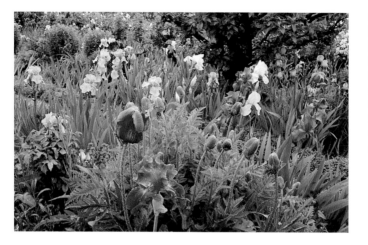

Left The hirsute green buds and fern-like foliage of the oriental poppy (*Papaver orientale*) are at first inconspicuous among the irises, until they burst into vivid flower to compete in a glorious summer kaleidoscope.

ened Monet's mood swings and deeply affected his ability to work. Yet he continued to garden. Throughout World War I, though within earshot of the sounds of battle, the garden remained an oasis of tranquillity, in which the seasonal patterns of cultivation still continued unchanged. The nearby field hospitals went on receiving fresh produce from the Maison Bleue.

In 1916, Monet constructed his third studio, to the east of the house. This provided a vast space in which he planned to re-create the water garden on canvas. The beauty and calm of this garden was to inspire Monet in his memorial to the dead: on 12 November 1918 he wrote to Clemenceau offering two painted panels of water lilies as his own tribute to France and its losses.

Alone or accompanied, to the end of his life Monet walked two or three times each day around his garden. In the 1920s,

flowers to paint when the weather's bad… I won't lay my brushes aside any more.'

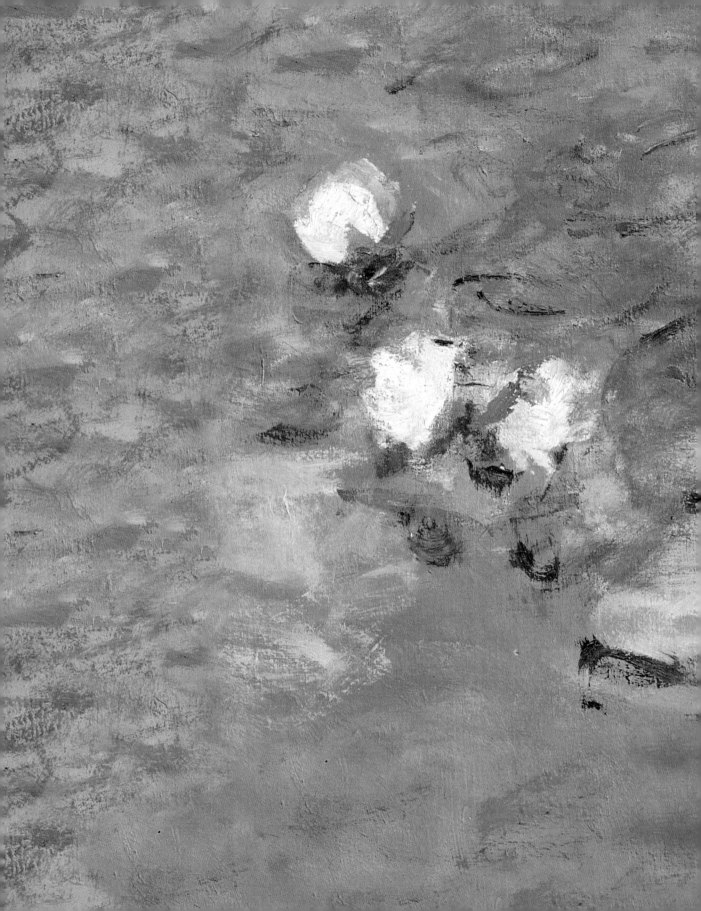

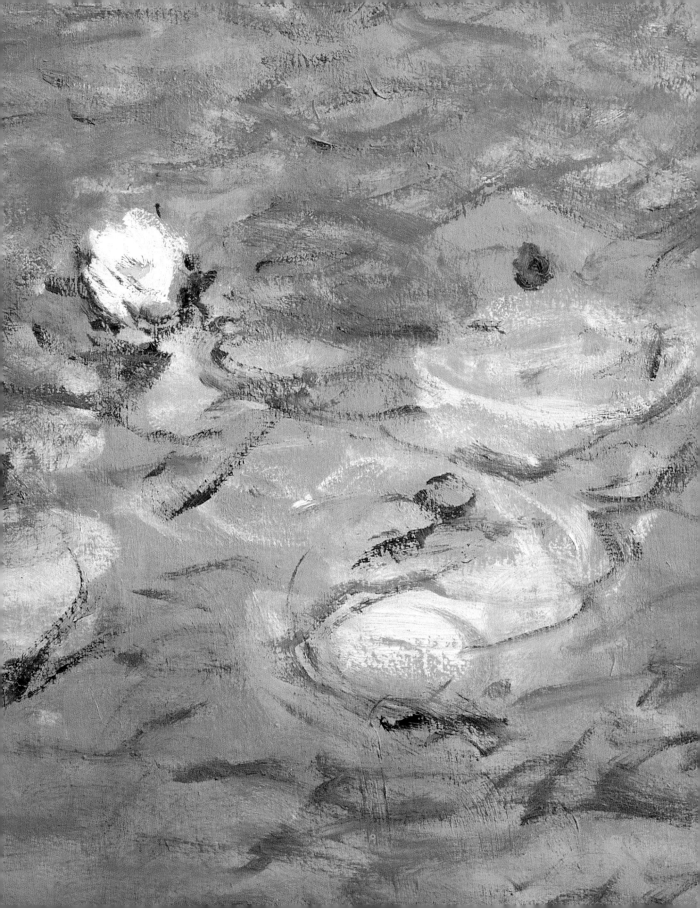

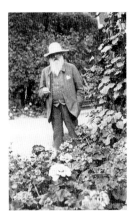

Clemenceau and Geffroy, as his dearest friends, described such walks taken in the company of the old man.

Let us go into the water garden with Clemenceau: 'A gate leads you across the road and railway line ... hidden by large rhododendrons and a tall trellis of climbing roses ... a silent pool decorated with dazzling water lilies leading under a wisteria swathed arch over the Japanese Bridge as pretty as a picture – sole concession to romanticism here. Alongside the railway line tall poplars, the pendulous branches of the weeping willows ... a peninsular of tall, dense bamboo, jungle ringed by the flow of swift water winding through the cheerful grasses. The circular path lined with trellises of climbing roses form arches of bright colours that open out onto the green meadows which extend right to the banks of the Seine.'

Geffroy, the younger chronicler of the two, wrote: 'Immediately that you push open the door ... you are entering

Previous page Away from the shade of the marginal plants, the sun warms the crisp white flowers and rich yellow centres of the lilies in this detail from **Water Lilies: Morning**, *c.*1925.

Left Monet in natural habitat, surrounded by the flowers and foliage of his garden. The variety of textures and shapes is enhanced by the black and white photograph of *c.*1913.

Right In painting and in his garden Monet based his composition on a series of horizontal planes with no vanishing point. The deep oranges of the wallflower draw the eye to the right, along the aubretia and over the elegant hoops of the Grande Allée.

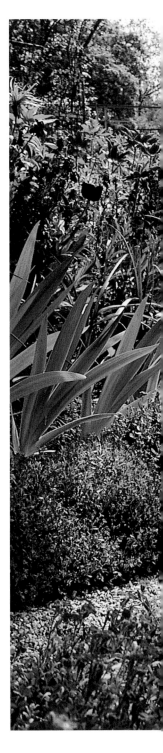

'What he loves in life and demands from it consists of one thing; to be in peace, to be left alone, to live peacefully within the bosom of his family, to be able to stay in his garden and tend his flowers without being disturbed.'

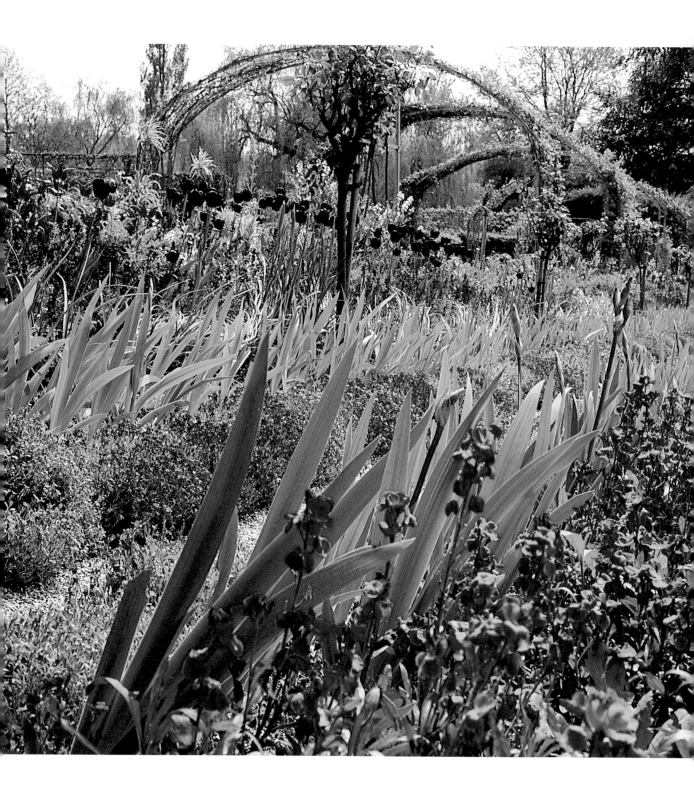

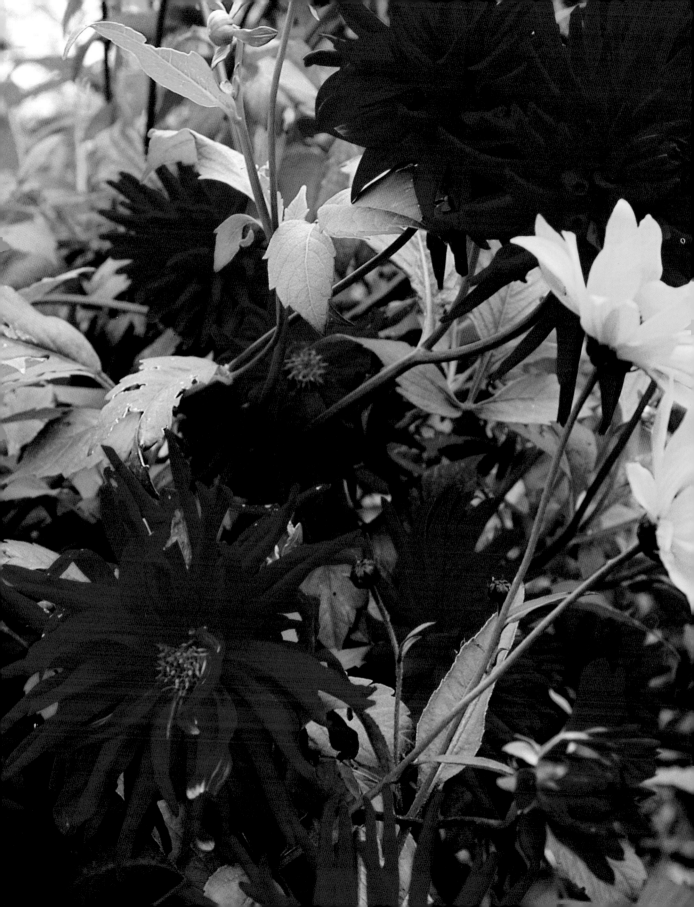

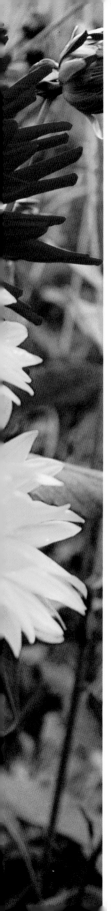

paradise. A kingdom brightened and sweetened with flowers. Every month celebrated with flowers from lilacs and irises to chrysanthemums and nasturtiums. Azaleas, hydrangeas, foxgloves, hollyhocks, forget-me-nots, violets, sumptuous and humble flowers mingle and thrive in the well-prepared earth, admirably cared

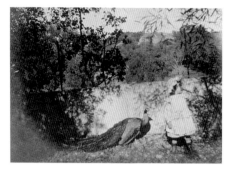

Above Monet's stepgranddaughter Sizi Salerou with one of the garden's peacocks. Sound was an important stimulus to the senses at Giverny, which was full of the songs and colours of tame and wild birds.

for by highly skilled gardeners, under the infallible eye of the master. If it is the rose season, all the wonders of glorious names engulf you with their shades and perfumes. There are rose trees, rose bushes, in hedges, on espaliers, wall climbers, trained to pillars and over the arches of the central *allée*. There are the very rare roses and the common but not necessarily less beautiful, single roses, sprays of eglantines, the deepest and the palest hues.'

Two months before he died, Monet wrote his last letter to Clemenceau, on 1 September 1926. His appetite had improved, he was sleeping well and he was still preparing himself to paint and do further work in the garden. But on 6 December he died at Giverny with Clemenceau, Blanche and Michel at his side. At the funeral, his gardeners carried the coffin. There was no oration or service, the dormant garden being sufficient witness to the life and death of its creator.

One of the most elegiac portraits of the water garden, effectively an epitaph, was written in 1933 by Stephen Gwynn for the British magazine *Country Life*: 'Flowers in a land garden hold all the attention; but here they live in a medium subtly penetrated with colour far down into its depths offering to the painter's brush problems of bewildering intricacy, and to the eye a tangle of delights.' This poetic evocation of the garden's water lilies, day lilies, agapanthus and willows was matched by photographs of the pond whose crystal serenity enticed the imagination into its reflective, fathomless depths.

Left Monet and his friend Caillebotte were both enthusiastic growers of dahlias. The nurseryman Georges Truffaut was impressed by the crosses Monet achieved at Giverny from the artist's favourite *Dahlia* 'Etoile de Digoin'.

The Paintings

Capturing the vision

THE RIVER SEINE was a presence that flowed alongside the whole of Monet's life, from his birth on 14 November 1840 in the narrow streets of Paris, before the impact of Haussmann had been realized, to his death at Giverny 86 years later.

In 1845 his family moved to Le Havre, at the river's mouth, the first of several locations on the lower reaches of the Seine that were to be such an influence on Monet's work. By his teens, the boy's talent had declared itself well enough for him to be earning pocket money through selling caricatures; M Louis Francois Nicolaie (1855) unconsciously foretells Monet's future passion for horticulture as its subject emerges from a potted rose bush. Within a year he was being encouraged by the landscape artist Eugène Boudin to paint outdoors and become a *plein airiste*, an ambition much helped by the recent introduction of oil paint in tubes. Boudin's technique of expressing light by a predominantly blond tonality known as *peinture claire* was central to Monet's own development of colour practice. Decades later, on 22 August 1892, Monet wrote to him from Giverny: 'I haven't forgotten that you were the first to teach me to see and understand.' Gatherings with other local landscape artists, at Ferme Saint-Siméon in Honfleur, also initi-

Below The willows at Giverny produce a canopy of green in high summer, echoed in the gently stirring waters of the pond. The weather was not always so benign, however, and Monet was devastated when freak storms in August 1910 ripped up his finest willows whilst in full leaf.

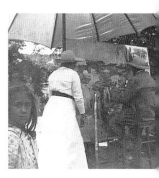

Above After the deaths of both Alice and Jean, Monet's widowed daughter-in-law Blanche assumed responsibility for his artistic needs. The child Nitia Salerou is a reminder that, despite recent events, Giverny remained the centre of the family.

Right The changing face of the water lily pond was a source of endless fascination to Monet. He loved watching the lilies unfurl and close up at dawn and evening; this detail from **Water Lilies: Morning**, c.1925, shows the plants on the point of opening in response to the rising sun.

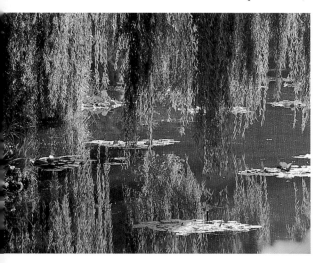

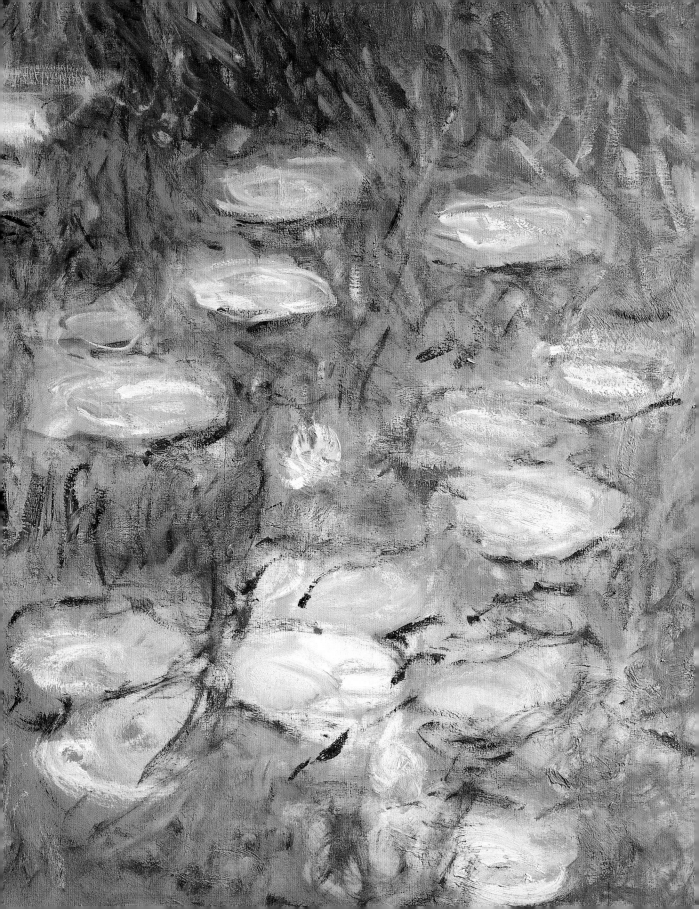

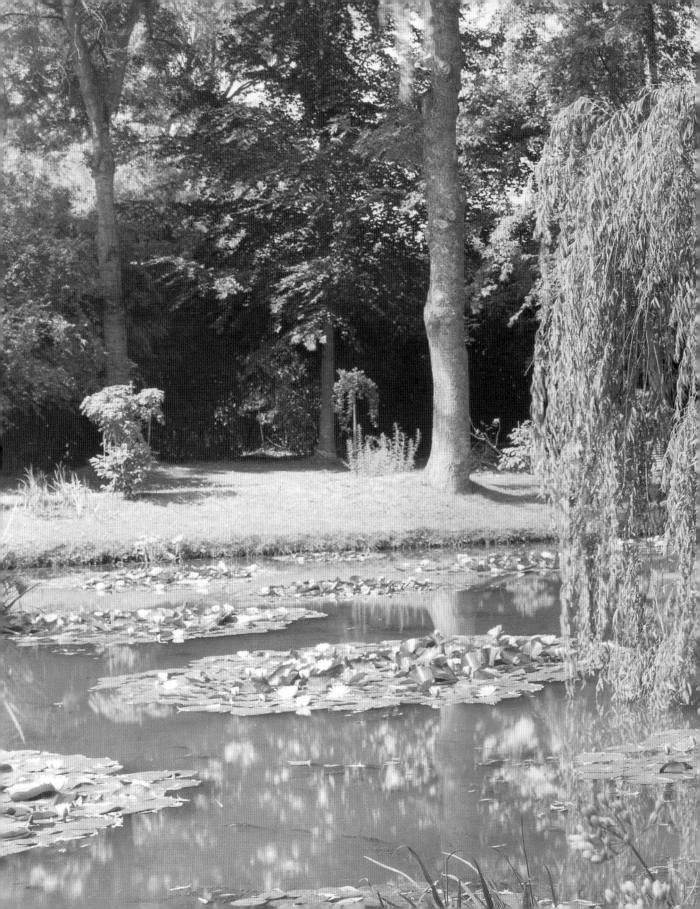

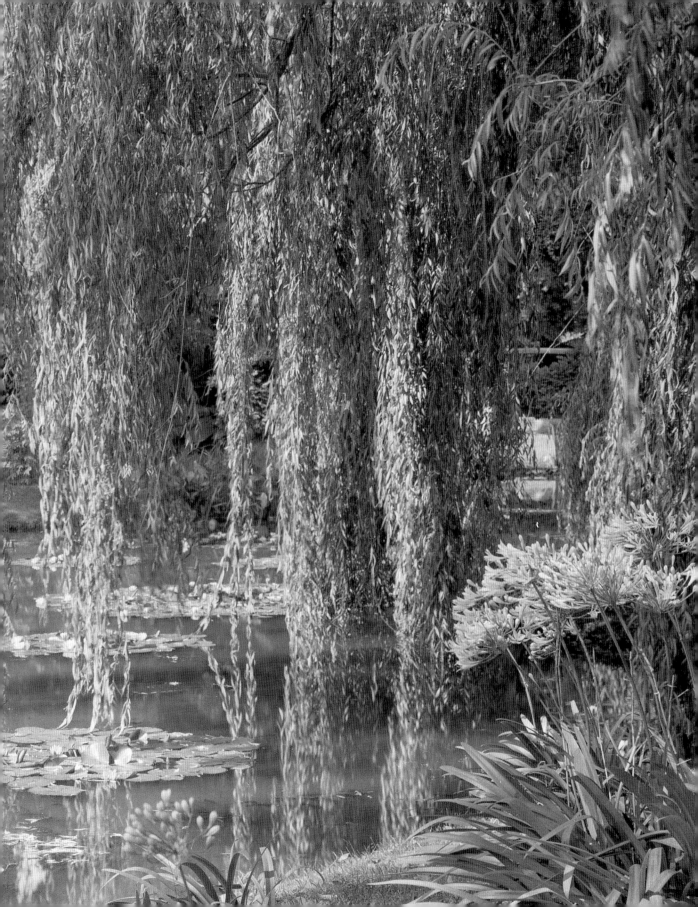

ated and nurtured Monet's tastes as a gourmand. In his early career Monet also painted in Paris, where the collection of his work in the Musée Marmottan, formerly a private *haut-bour-geois* home, includes the famous urban scene of *Impression, Sunrise*. It was among a group of paintings exhibited in 1874 that were sarcastically described by the critic Louis Leroy as an 'Exhibition of Impressionists', incapable of producing finished work. The independent artists thus referred to adopted the name to identify their movement, a tag which endured.

Throughout his career, Monet mostly painted close to home (and water), with the exception of the period immediately after his arrival at Giverny in 1883. His travels encompassed a spectacular range of natural features and light values, from the warmth in the Mediterranean light of his Bordighera paintings to the crash of relentless waves against the rocks of Belle Ile. As early as 1867, the *Terrace at Sainte-Adresse*, portraying his elegant father and his Aunt Lecadre, exemplified the brilliance in his youthful paintings and anticipated an ability to capture fleeting movements and reflections, described by him as *l'instantaneité*. Later, as physical objects diminished in importance to him he tirelessly sought to capture the *enveloppe*, the outward transitory play of light.

Monet's changing vision

All senses are subjective. We can understand Monet's assertion that he fell in love with the ray of light and the reflection, and have experienced dramatic effects of light – shafts of sunlight through dark clouds or particles of dust in rays streaming through glass. However, we can never be certain of his own immediate perceptions. Again and again contemporaries expressed themselves astounded by his sensitivity to light, and indeed the observation of successive seasons at Giverny enabled Monet to appreciate the most minute changes in the colours of the *enveloppe*. Though mood swings

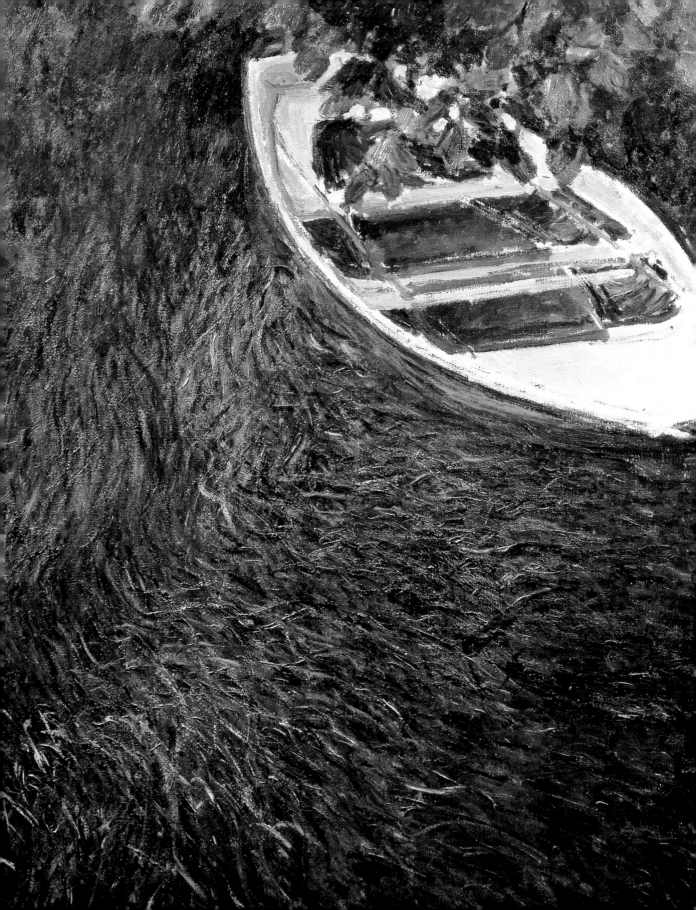

Right A tributary of the Epte, the tiny River Ru was diverted to create Monet's water garden when he acquired an irregularly shaped piece of land across the road from his existing garden in 1893. Sluices controlled the water flow in and out of the pond. At the garden's west end the planting is wilder, retaining the illusion of an unaltered stream.

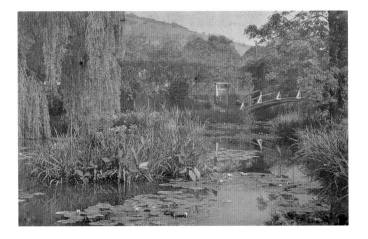

dominated his domestic life, triggered by artistic frustration (especially with the weather), these were not reflected in the scenic nuances of feeling he sought to express in his motifs. The move to Giverny marks the start of Monet's obsession with such nuances of effect and atmosphere. He captured them using brushwork inspired by Delacroix's style and, like Manet, by the Japanese use of line and luminous colour. One interesting detail following the move to Giverny was the change in his signature, which thereafter became matched to the colour scheme of his paintings.

The characteristic poplars, the skilled rural craft expressed in the neighbourhood's grain stacks and the nearby haze of fruit blossom and fields of poppies all drew Monet to the surroundings of Giverny. It was these that led him on the first steps towards the creation of his pool, whose water lilies evoke the ancient conceit of water nymphs. The hundreds of paintings executed after his arrival at Giverny share a long, labyrinthine journey to the central paradise of his garden.

Right An unusual and possibly unfinished interpretation, **Water Lily Pond: The Bridge** emphasizes the play of foliage reflections on the surface of the pond. Dancing pink water lilies complement the soft yellow light.

' To me, the motif itself is an insignificant factor; what I

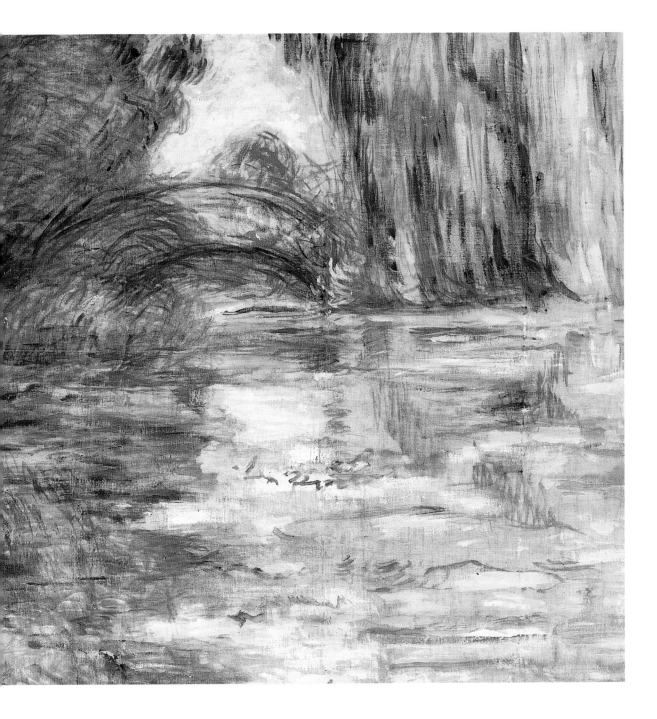

want to reproduce is what lies between the motif and me.'

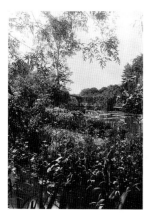

Throughout, he was obsessed by momentary sensations of light, reflecting the influence of painters such as Corot and Turner and moving away from the jostling themes of smart urban France as he sought to represent the colours and moods of untrammelled nature. However, the inspired *plein airiste* always had a studio. Initially it was a barn, succeeded in 1897 by his second studio, and in 1916 the great third studio was constructed.

Monet's early years at Giverny bore witness to a more hard-nosed commercial approach to his work, as he encouraged rivalry between dealers and pushed for higher prices. Between 1886 and 1890 there was a rift in his relationship with Durand-Ruel, and when business resumed between them it was on Monet's terms. He used several other dealers meanwhile; in 1888 he made a contract with Boussod & Valadon through their branch manager Théo van Gogh, brother to Vincent, for an exhibition of his Antibes paintings. On seeing one of Vincent van Gogh's iris paintings, Monet commented: 'How could a man who has so loved flowers and light and has rendered them so well, have managed to be so unhappy?'

Figures in the landscape

The eight children of the Giverny household, including the four teenage girls, provided dynamic opportunities for figure painting, but few of the resulting pictures were signed and dated, suggesting either that they were not meant to be sold or that Monet remained dissatisfied with them. *Poppy Field near Giverny* of 1885 is dominated by varied textures of grass and foliage, and *Spring at Giverny* of 1886 by an effusion of blossom and branches. A similar emphasis appears in a picture Monet

Left Along the edge of his pool, Monet used marginal plants and bushes as a lacy screen through which to glimpse the glittering water. Where foliage and flowers overhung the water, their reflections contributed to the serenity of the scene.

Right In 1886, three years after his household settled at Giverny, Monet painted **Springtime**, a portrait of his son Jean with Suzanne Hoschedé under a canopy of apple blossom. The atmosphere of burgeoning romance proved to be Monet's wishful thinking.

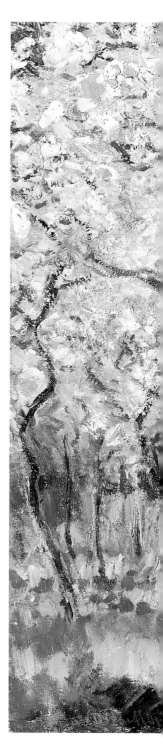

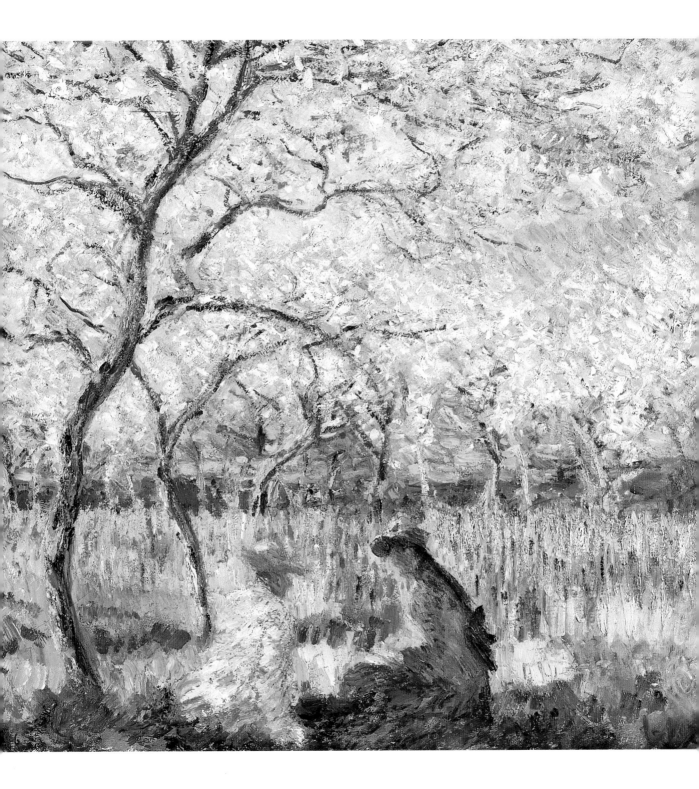

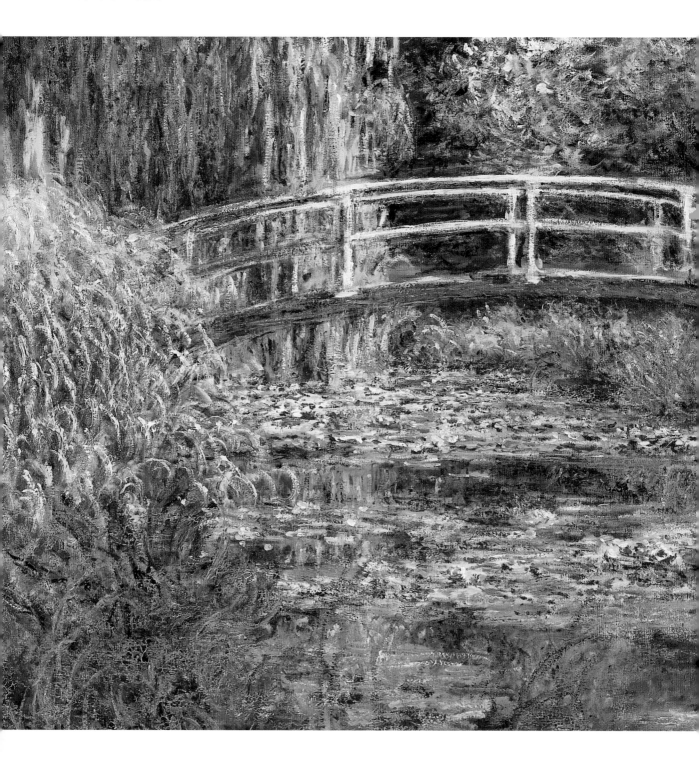

admired at the Royal Academy whilst in London during July 1887, John Singer Sargent's *Carnation, Lily, Lily, Rose*. Here two young girls absorbed in lighting Chinese lanterns are framed by lilies, carnations and waving grasses. In the following month, he described in a letter to the critic Théodore Duret how he was experimenting with painting figures in the open air as if they were landscapes. Thus family members appear in many paintings at this time, but not as central themes. Monet's favourite model was Suzanne, whose appearance,

Left The original bridge was a simple structure, in keeping with the smaller pond that it served. Both are shown here in **The Water Lily Pond** (**Symphony in Rose**), 1900, where the delicately curling foliage and soft pink notes of the water lilies present a peaceful, harmonious setting. The pond's surface later tripled in size, and a canopy was added to the bridge to support the creeping wisteria.

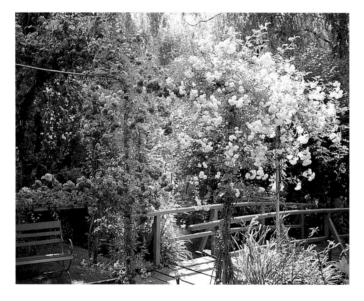

Left The rose arches by the pond provide a delightful arbour. They feature in several of Monet's paintings, sometimes in bold, powerful colours.

when he began to paint her in *Woman with a Parasol* (1886), gave no suspicion of how shocked he would be by her resemblance in the picture to his first wife, Camille.

According to contemporary gossip, the type of voluptuous nude favoured by Renoir was certainly met with disapproval by Alice Hoschedé. Monet, too, had his criticisms. Renoir's *Bather* (1892), which hung over Monet's bed, reportedly provoked his comment to a guest: 'Yes, the nude is beautiful, but see how sadly conventional the landscape is...'. In 1889, the major Monet-Rodin retrospective took place under the direction of Georges Petit of Petit Bros at the Hôtel Buron in Paris.

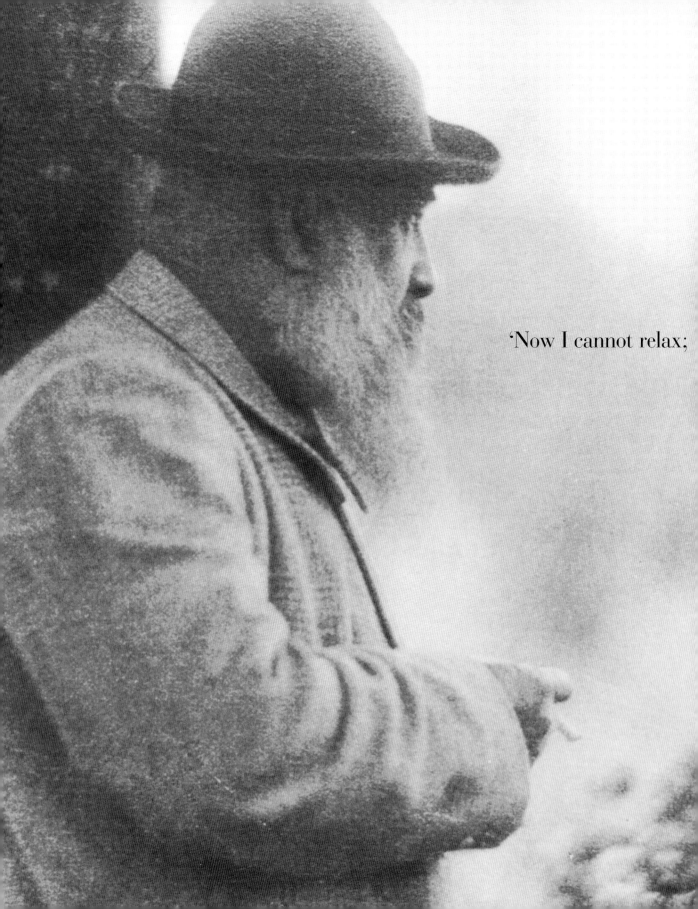

'Now I cannot relax;

This exhibition, staged to coincide with the Exposition Universelle, at last provided the commercial break Monet needed; and four of the paintings on display, termed by him '*Essais de figures en plein air*', also gave a glimpse of what was to come – the artist's emphasis on landscape over figure painting. Figures, members of Monet's family, drift asymmetrically in meadows, gardens or on the river, buoyant in the flecks and dashes of colour that he applied to his landscapes. Boats loom into the picture like those in a Japanese print, whilst the eye is

colours pursue me like a constant worry ... even ... in my sleep.'

drawn into the waterweeds that move just below the surface. In the exhibition catalogue introduction, Octave Mirbeau wrote: 'Between our eye and the appearance of figures, seas, flowers and fields, the air intervenes in a real sense. The air visibly bathes every object, endows it with mystery, envelops it with all the colours, muted or dazzling, that it has picked up before reaching our eyes.'

At the same time, Monet started to concentrate on using white primed canvas, which established a softly luminous quality, as he said 'to establish my scale of values', and, only occasionally, toned primers. By degrees the figures in Monet's works became subsumed into the landscape; after 1890, he ceased painting them altogether as his attention turned to two features – the grain stacks and, a year later, the poplar trees – that typified the countryside around Giverny. Geffroy noted in his preface for the exhibition of May 1891 that it was Monet's efforts to capture all the nuances of light and seasonal effects on the grain stacks that had brought an end to his travels.

Flower paintings at Giverny

On arrival at Giverny, one of the family's first tasks was gardening, for sustenance in two senses. They needed fruit, herbs

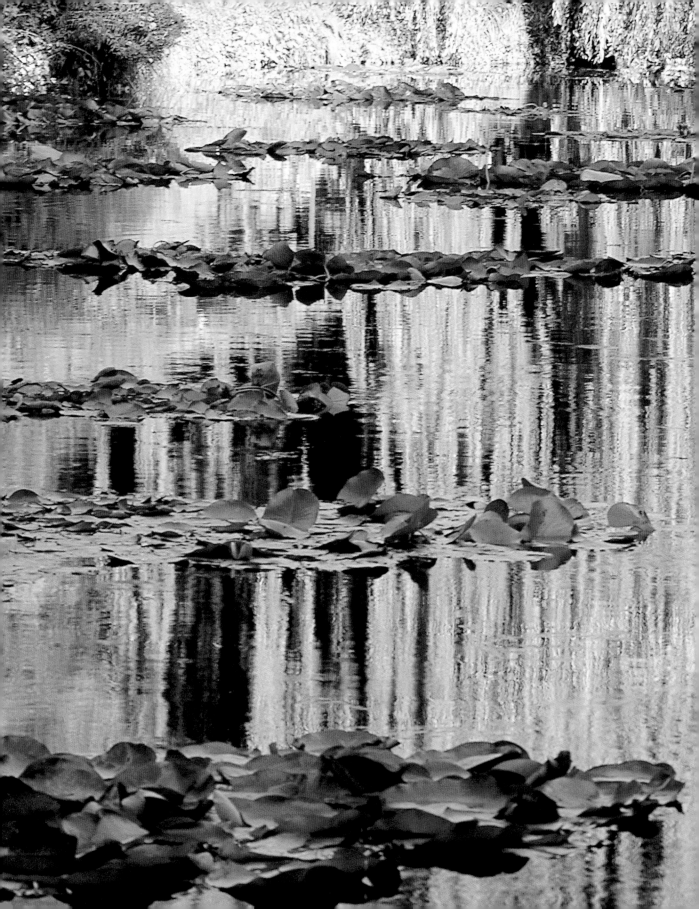

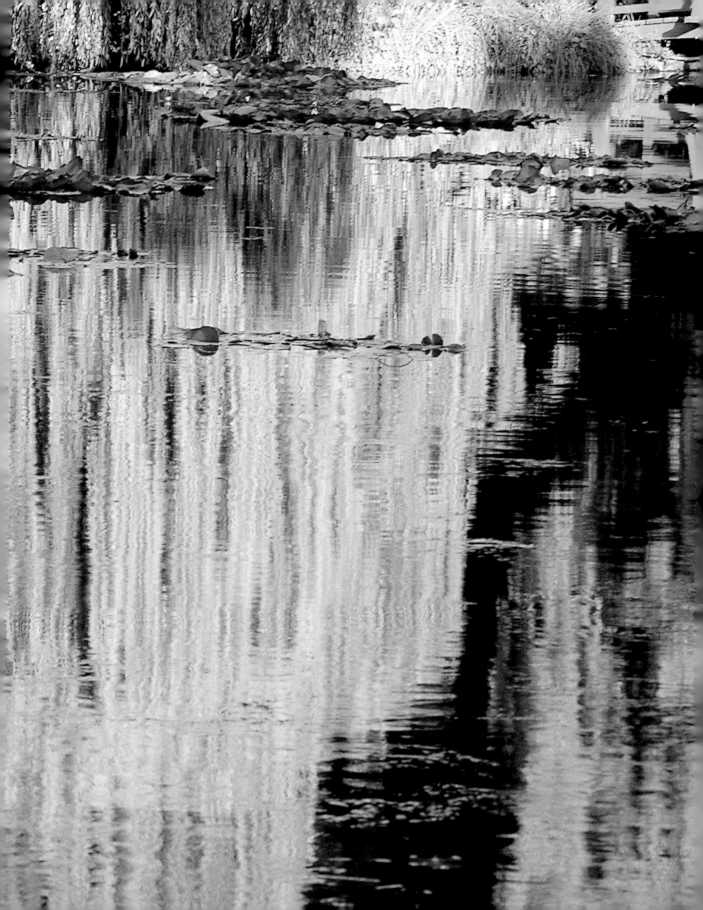

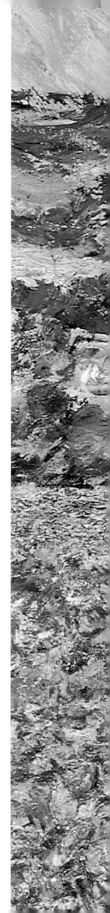

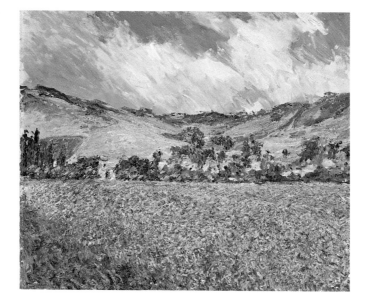

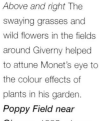

Above and right The swaying grasses and wild flowers in the fields around Giverny helped to attune Monet's eye to the colour effects of plants in his garden. **Poppy Field near Giverny**, 1885, places the glorious colours of a local meadow in the context of the region's steep, embracing hills.

and vegetables to eat; and they also required flowers to be painted on wet days as a source of income – although in fact 18 months elapsed before Monet actually painted any of his home-grown blooms. Geffroy wrote of the other uses for Monet's first 'barn' studio, attached to the house, 'that he cleans up, that he completes, that he harmonizes' his paintings there. The earliest, uncharacteristic, evidence of plants from the Giverny garden as subject matter are the still lifes painted for the six panels of Durand-Ruel's dining room doors; these depict poppies, sunflowers, Christmas roses, jonquils, gladioli, dahlias, tulips and carnations in pots. In 1893, Caillebotte had painted *Chrysanthemums*, showing flowers from his garden at Petit Gennevilliers, which Monet purchased after the artist's death in 1894. Monet's own four canvases depicting chrysanthemums, executed in 1896–7, portray opulent blooms jostling towards the light, with brushwork that captures the petals' shaggy texture and colour harmonies. Compared to work by the Japanese master Hokusai or by Caillebotte, whose flowers seem respectively airborne and firmly rooted in the soil, Monet's chrysanthemums appear to float on the canvas.

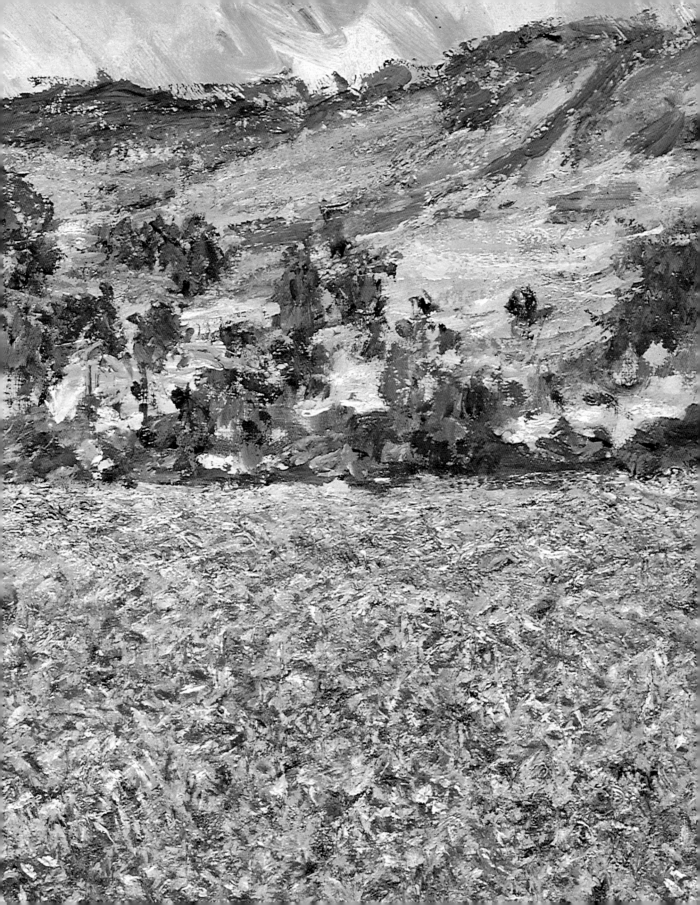

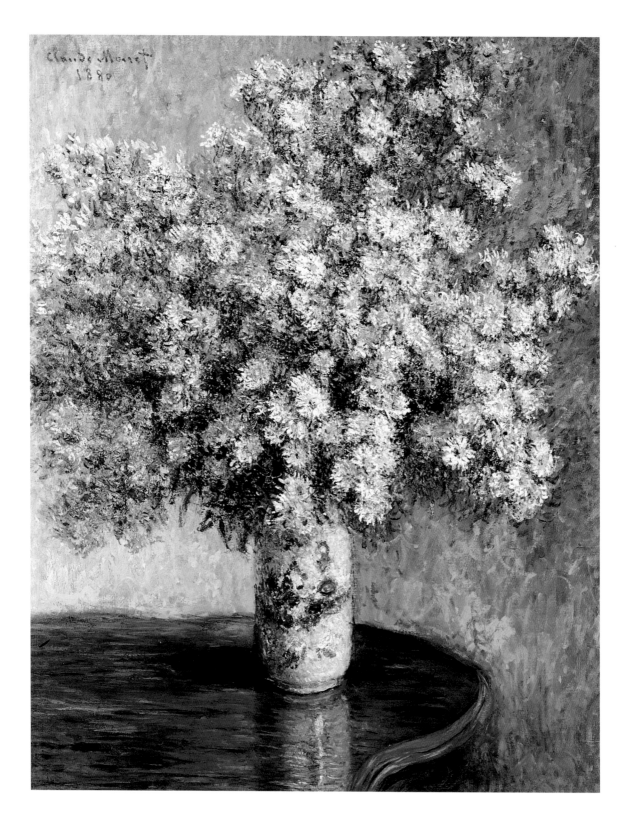

The Impressionists and French society

It was not entirely from motives of altruism that Monet, during the year following the 1889 Exposition Universelle, became obsessed with raising a subscription for Manet's 1863 *Olympia*. Acceptance by the State of this controversial canvas forced a review of previous condemnations and made a move towards recognizing the Impressionists' worth. It also helped revive the tradition of encouragement for avant-garde paint-

'alone in his solitude and remoteness, he maintains the integrity of his personality.'

ing in France – a movement of which Monet was currently a part. Monet's organization of the subscription and his negotiations with the authorities showed not only skill in diplomacy but also political prowess, dexterously sowing the seeds for his own place in French history.

His deftness in public matters was matched by steadfastness in patterns of work. Following the 1889 retrospective, a new friendship was formed with Lilla Cabot Perry, who became a neighbour at Giverny. In 1927, after Monet's death, she wrote of their discussions on painting methods: 'The man himself, his gruff honesty, his disarming sincerity, his sensitive and warm nature, amazed us as much as his paintings, and this first meeting marked the start of a friendship which brought us back ten summers to Giverny.' He told her that the placing on canvas of each leaf on a tree was as important as the positioning of the eyes, nose or mouth on a face. She gently ribbed him but accepted his instructions: 'When you go out to paint, try to forget what object you have before you, a tree, a house, a field or whatever. Merely think, here is a little square of blue, here an oblong of pink, here a streak of yellow, and paint it just as it looks to you, the exact colour and shape, until it gives your own naive impression of the scene before you.'

Left Still lifes had formed part of Monet's work since his early years in Paris – partly due to financial pressures, as it avoided the expense of hired models. Later, at Giverny, they could be undertaken in poor weather, giving Monet the opportunity to study individual flowers away from a garden context. *Chrysanthemums*, 1880, anticipates the fascination with petal texture and shading shown in the four still-life canvases of 1897.

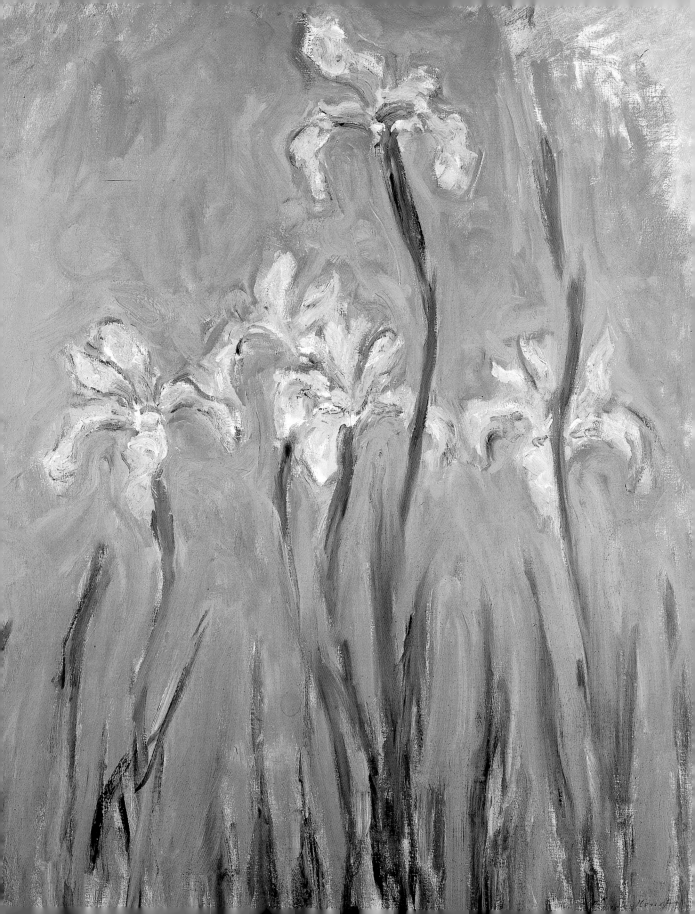

Left The shape of the flowerheads on their tall, upright stems dominates the composition of **Yellow Irises**, 1924–5. The effects of light on the moving subject is explored in a manner similar to Monet's representations of the poplars around Giverny. Symbols of French rural prosperity, the trees provided Monet with a frequently recurring motif.

Right Monet was fascinated by the esoteric qualities of irises and orchids. His intense involvement with the flowers enabled him to spot a dead flowerhead in borders such as this at a hundred paces, despite increasingly poor eyesight.

As a memento of his own resistance to fashion, on the wall of his first studio at Giverny, later the family sitting room, Monet made a point of hanging his *Sunrise at Vétheuil*, painted in the early 1870s. He had tried to sell it for 50 francs to one of his first benefactors, the baritone Faure, in 1873. Faure's reaction had been to comment ' ... yes, the Seine, and then the mist which, in the first rays of light, clouds the view. You can't see very well. But I suppose it's the mist's fault. All the same, there is not enough to make a picture. Put a bit more into the picture, and then I will happily buy the painting.' Monet did no such thing. In 1879 the painting was on his easel when Faure paid a visit; the enchanted singer offered 600 francs for such 'a haze of clarity'. As a wry reminder of fickle public taste, Monet kept the painting for himself.

The composition of patterns

The importance to Monet of each painting's design and make-up was paramount. In place of the established format of high-toned foreground receding into the distance, he sought *l'instantaneité* of a flash of aware-ness within a single moment in the land-scape. He looked for patterns, as Theodore Robinson recalled in 1892, of 'leafage against the sky' and 'reflections', that is, motifs supplied by his garden. This is apparent in the climbing roses against a blue sky of *Roses*, his painting of the light and shade on stands of irises, and the inspiration for the many bridge and water lily paintings. Much is made of Monet's interest in, and collection of, Japanese prints. Emphatically not a copy-ist, his ideas in this as in many other inter-ests were informed and stimulated by an

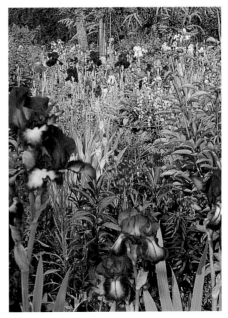

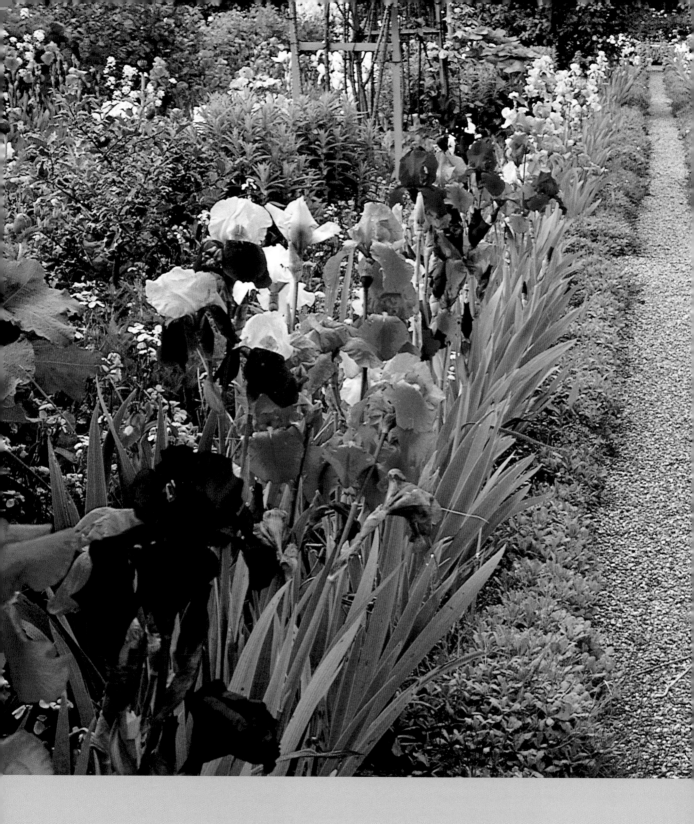

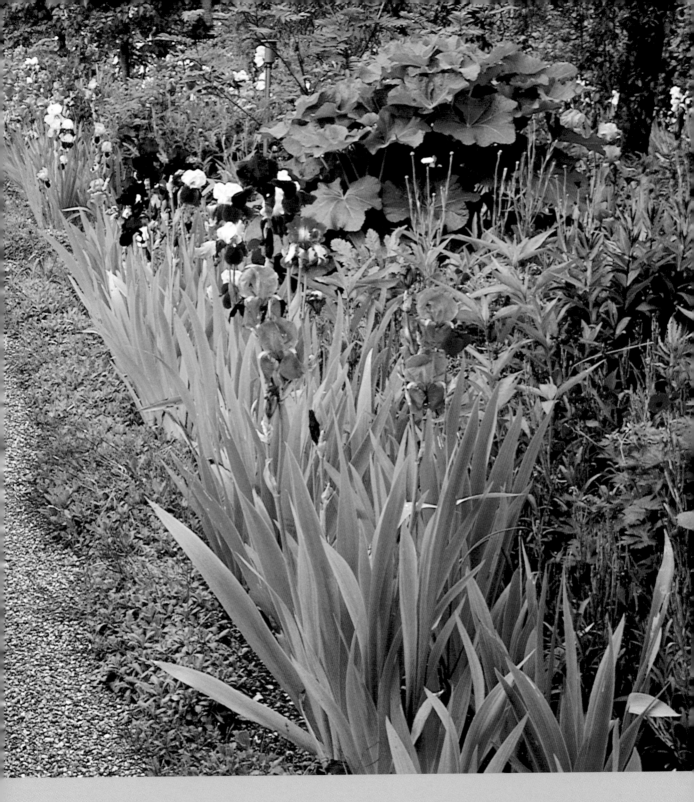

'A garden with flowers, that is all he desires.'

intelligent appraisal. Pissarro wrote in 1893: 'Admirable, the Japanese exhibition. Hiroshige is a marvellous Impressionist. Monet, Rodin and I are all full of enthusiasm for it ... these Japanese artists confirm me in our visual standpoint.'

The clearest Japanese parallels in Monet's paintings are seen in the 'Bridge' and 'Water Lilies' series, of which the former motif reflects the device of Hiroshige's *Wisteria* and the latter that of Hokusai's *Women Gathering Water Lilies*, part of Monet's collection. In these series, the extended horizontals of

' ... it resembles no other, first because **it consists only of the simplest flowers** and then because they grow to unheard-of heights.'

the water lilies, punctuated by willows, are in the tradition of Japanese screen painting, where a single scene is carried across several panels, sometimes broken with close-up trees. By 1897, Monet was himself discussing the project of a continuous horizontal painting as decoration for a circular reception or dining room.

Losing the horizon

With the exception of the Grande Allée, Monet rejected customary linear perspectives in designing his gardens, and the same was true of his paintings, apart from those of the early 'Japanese Bridge' series. In his work, depth and space are shown by overlapping successive planes, by not focusing on distant objects and by playing with the horizon. It is said that Monet never sacrificed space to pattern, but experimented with his compositions in the hope of achieving both. He burnt many canvases that did not satisfy him, but fortunately undertook nothing more severe in his gardening than dextrous pruning and clever planting.

In botanical terms, could the relationship between Monet's

Right The height of Monet's rich tapestry of flowers was often remarked by his contemporaries. Here, common marguerites and the glorious orange 'Fire King' wallflowers weave their way through the hooks and dashes of irises, widely used in Giverny as architectural accents.

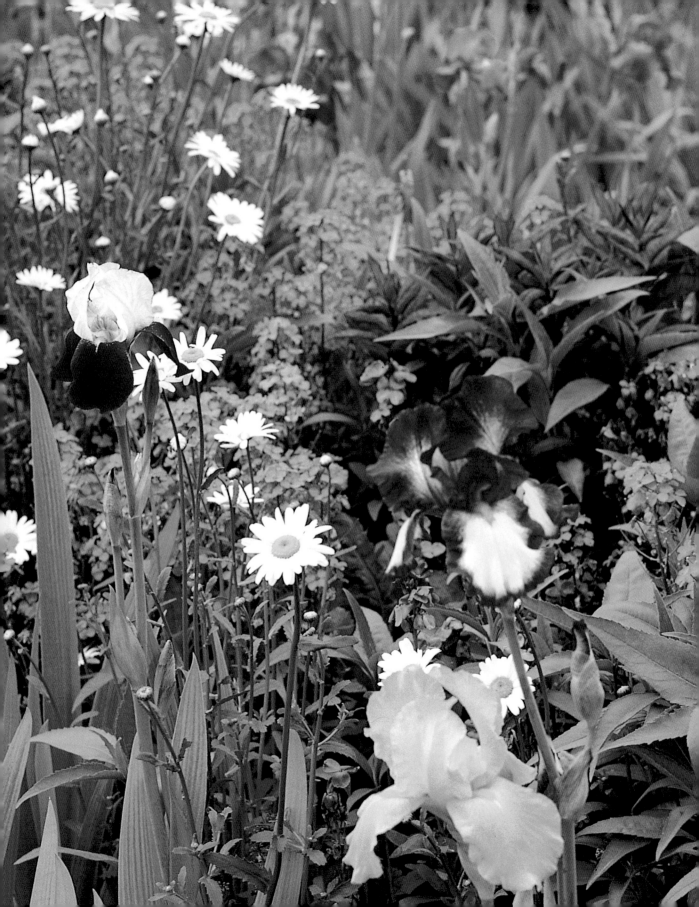

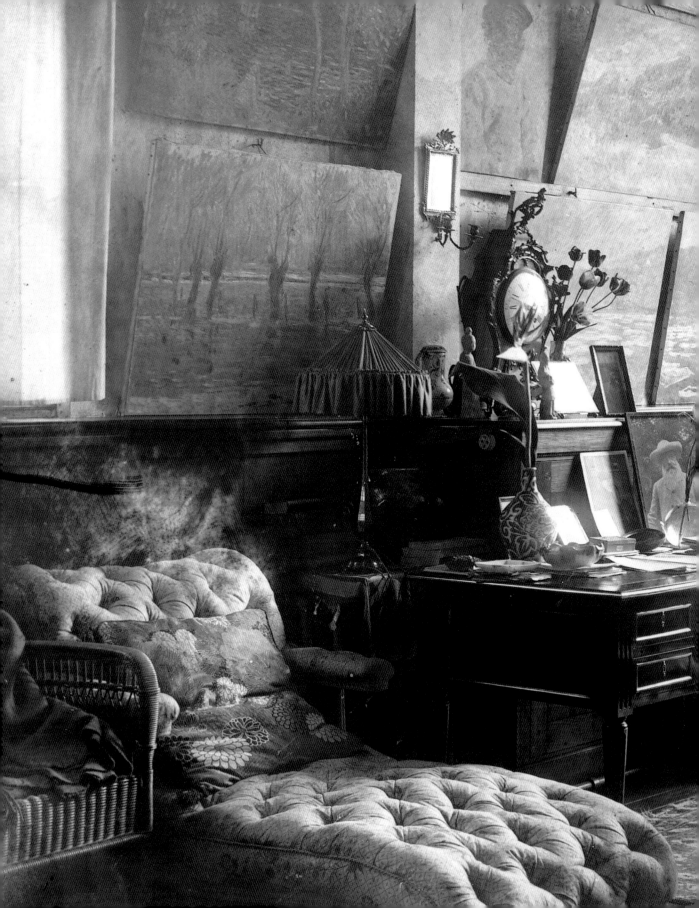

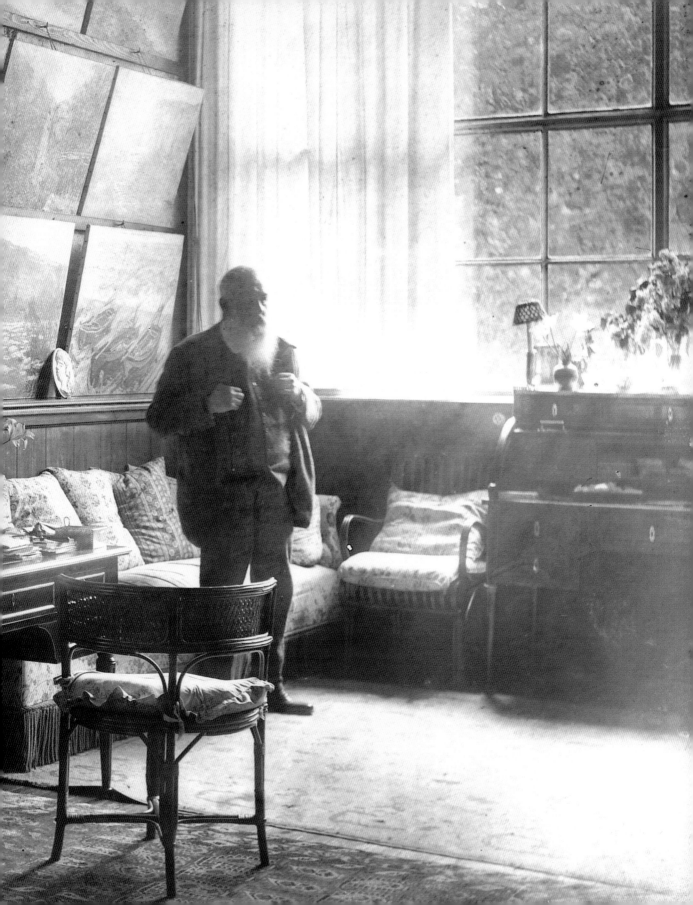

garden and his paintings most appropriately be described as osmotic or symbiotic? On the one hand, he might be seen to represent the stronger substance that drew gardening, the weaker one, through the membrane of his painting. On the other hand, it may be that his garden and his paintings had a symbiotic existence, governed by mutual dependence. Whatever the method, the results produced an extraordinary domain where colour and pattern were a magnet to family and friends alike; one in which nature, diligently husbanded, appeared as a source of all goodness and wisdom.

The first 'Water Lily' canvases

On 15 January 1900, Monet wrote to Paul Durand-Ruel to confirm that he was sending two crates of pictures worth 45,000 francs for display at the Paris World Fair. One crate held six paintings from the 'Water Lilies' series; the second, a further 'Water Lily' picture plus one other for Geffroy. These first pictures of Monet's water garden, painted between 1897 and 1900, contrast natural textures and colours, capturing the water lilies in a manner that echoes the painting of his early

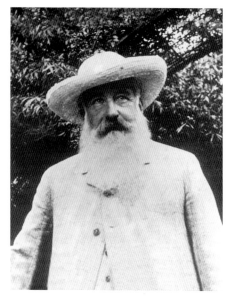

Giverny spring blossoms. The Japanese Bridge is a pristine shape spanning the water lilies that gleam on the pool below. As a subject, however, the water garden was set aside for a while; in 1901, after tripling its length, Monet turned to the upper garden for inspiration while the new waterscaping matured.

The colours of the printed word

The Dreyfus affair divided France, and many in Monet's circle of friends shared a public reaction of disgust at what they saw as the corruption and cynicism of the

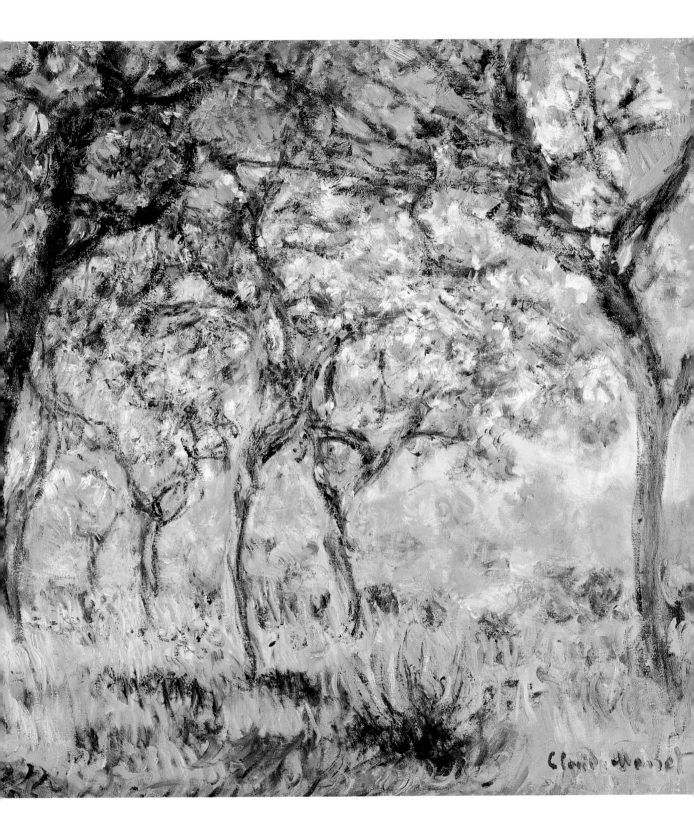

Claude Monet

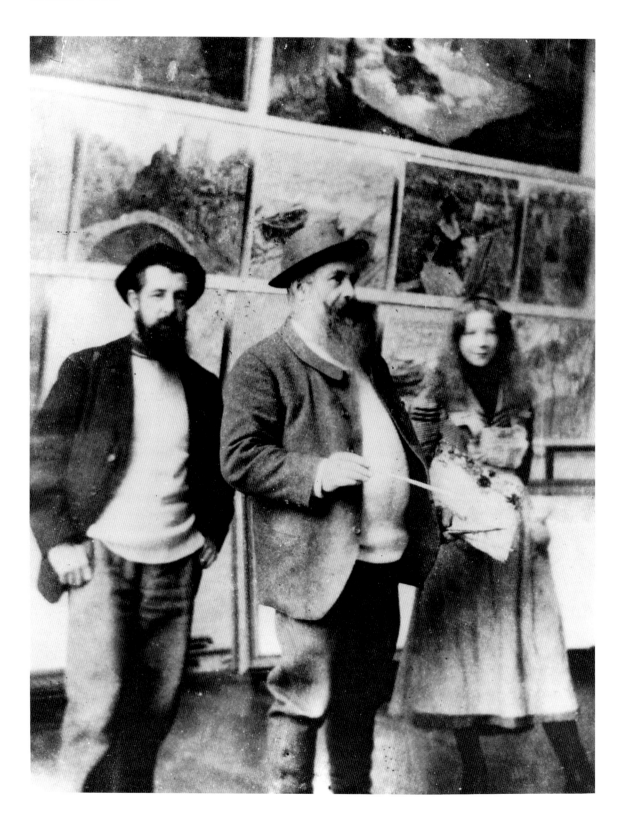

French government. Shortly afterwards, in 1899, Octave Mirbeau published *Jardin des supplices*, a Gothic horror story set in a garden rather like that at Giverny – not, however, the scene of flower-filled bowers that he and Monet had tended, but an apocalyptic version. In Mirbeau's tale, the trees of the central avenue are hollowed out to hold and torture bodies. A vast pool is edged with irises, diabolic flowers stained the colours of blood; and what look like water lilies are in fact morgue-white decapitated heads. Monet read this description of a garden fertilized by the blood of murdered prisoners and decorated with eroticized flowers and instruments of torture, and he seems to express something of its anger in the harsh colours of his upper garden paintings of 1901–2.

Left One of a series of informal family photographs taken in the second studio. Monet and Jacques Hoschedé are portrayed with Jacques' stepdaughter, Anna Bergman, during her visit in 1902.

A parallel between the gardens at Giverny and those in Shakespeare's plays was evoked by Geffroy in 1921. Some onlookers may see Monet as a magus, like Prospero in *The Tempest*, who purges an enchanted island of evil magic to effect peace and reconciliation. It is not hard to find Caliban, 'a man or a fish... his fins like arms', the 'savage and deformed slave' of the play, in the gnarled bark of the willows weeping into the pool. Geoffroy also describes Ariel, the play's 'airy spirit', as dancing like a will-o'-the-wisp over the pool's water lily buds. In its darker aspect, this phenomenon derives from graveyards, the gases emitted by decomposing bodies. The sorrows and evil of war are hauntingly encapsulated in Monet's *Weeping Willows* of 1918, against which must be balanced the peace and serenity of his commemorative water lily panels.

A series of water landscapes

When Monet exhibited 'The Water Lilies: a series of water landscapes' in 1909, these 48 canvases included the only tondi, or circular paintings, that he ever executed. Decorative in effect, and predominantly a wonderful blue, they give the impression of looking out of a porthole on a perfect summer's

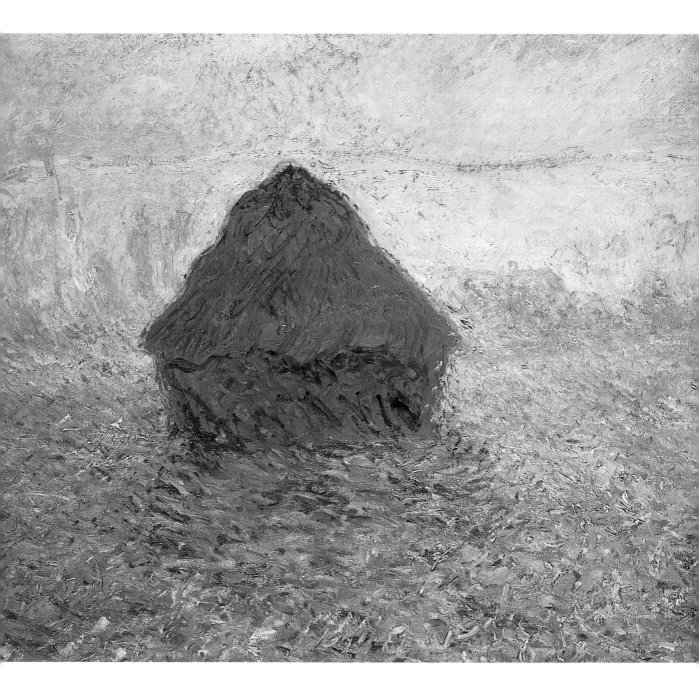

'One day, at Varengeville, I saw a little car arriving in a cloud of dust. Monet gets out of it, looks at the sun and consults his watch: 'I'm half an hour late,' he says, 'I'll come back tomorrow.''

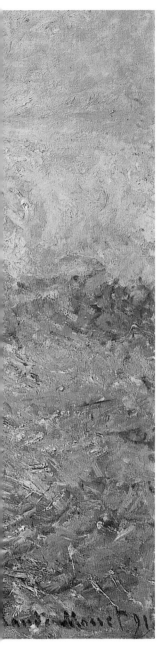

Left The grainstacks around Giverny provided a theme for Monet's first venture into 'series' painting in the 1890s. The motif, illustrated here in *Grainstacks, Hazy Sunshine*, 1891, became a vehicle through which to explore changing light effects in the Normandy countryside. It often involved work on several canvases over an afternoon, each reflecting a subtly different angle and quality of light.

Right Monet shared a love of cars with Clemenceau; as neighbours the two men frequently drove over to visit one another. Here Monet is portrayed in his Panhard-Levassor car, c.1901.

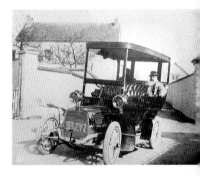

day. For this second water garden series, painted 1904–9, Monet focused on the surface of the pool, with the harmonies of blue and green and the reflected trees and clouds filling the canvas. He was prepared to leave a canvas unfinished until the weather ensured that the exact colour effects he had begun to paint returned – though in some cases this meant waiting a full year before a painting could be finished. Equally, he would destroy unsatisfactory works; in 1907 he told Durand-Ruel that he had burnt 'at least 30 of them to my great satisfaction'.

In the 'Water Lilies' series of 1904–9, the lily pads are at times redefined in bold loops of paint. This technique was developed by using brushwork that suggested fluid layers of paint over the areas representing water, so that the lilies appear to float across the surface of the picture. As John House writes: ' ... we can now appreciate the power of the brushstroke itself as a means of lyrical expression on a grand

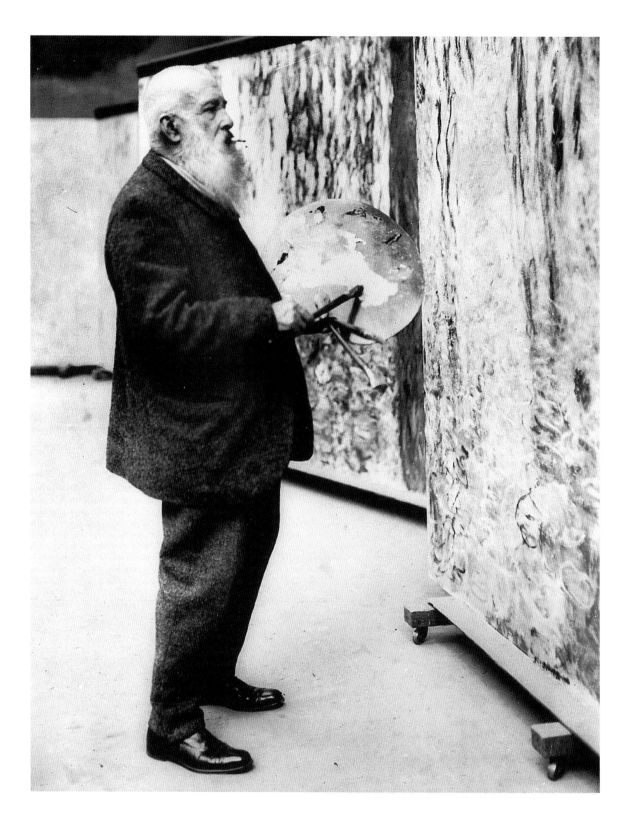

Left The great water lily canvases of the Grandes Décorations project were to occupy the last ten years of Monet's life. He worked on them intensively through World War I, constantly aware of his failing health and eyesight. In refusing an invitation to visit the art dealer Gustave Bernheim-Jeune, Monet was to note 'I don't have many years left to me and I have to devote all my time to painting, in the hope of achieving something worthwhile in the end.'

scale.' Such lyricism was achieved only after careful contemplation of the extended pool, planted with new and ever more colourful (and expensive) water lilies.

After 1912 Monet only painted summer subjects in his gardens. The winter months were spent in retouching and finishing his canvases, or sometimes in destroying them. Two years later, when he started his *Grandes Décorations*, he had attempted almost no huge canvas outdoors since his *Women in the Garden*, executed some 50 years earlier at Ville d'Avray. However, his

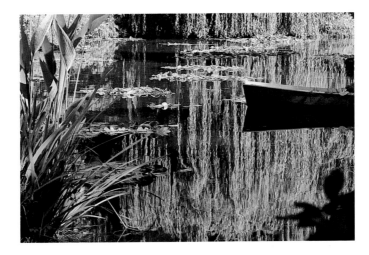

Left Not only Monet's gardeners sometimes worked from the boats; in the early days of his water garden he also painted some of his canvases from a vantage point on the pool. The precedent had been established earlier in his career by a 'studio boat' used at Argenteuil and Vétheuil; it inspired an affectionate painting by Edouard Manet in 1874.

vast third studio, built in 1916, enabled him to rework and elaborate his canvases, working from smaller studies made beside the pool.

Monet's sight

In late July 1912, Monet discovered that he could not see out of his right eye. A local specialist from Vernon diagnosed the early symptoms of cataract and urged a surgical operation. Unwilling to take the smallest gamble with his sight, Monet sought a second opinion from a doctor in Paris, who recommended specialist treatment. His sight did not deteriorate; in fact, by April 1913 he reported that it was clearer, but he had started wearing the now familiar straw hat to protect his eyes from bright sunshine. In July he began to paint his rose pergolas, incidentally providing a rare photo-opportunity for the magazine *Je sais tout*. Throughout World War I he kept on working. Michel Monet, Jean-Pierre Hoschedé and Albert Salerou fought in the conflict – Michel indeed was at Verdun during some of the most severe fighting of the war – but Monet's contribution was restricted to growing food for the local field hospitals and creating works of art.

The joy of the Armistice, with the acceptance by the nation of Monet's offer of two commemorative panels, was clouded in 1919 when his cataracts worsened. Clemenceau, originally trained as a doctor, beseeched Monet to have an operation, but nothing would induce him to risk impairing his vision further. Within the year, he told Geffroy that he could no longer work outside, and in January 1921 he confessed to a journalist that he had to have his paint tubes and brushes carefully laid out to avoid inadvertently mixing the colours. By May 1922, he was virtually blind.

At his wits' end, Clemenceau finally cajoled Monet into seeing a specialist, Dr Charles Coutela. The first part of a three-stage operation was fixed for November, but postponed to mid-January; it was taken further in late January and finished in July. Between each operation, Blanche nursed the irascible patient at Giverny. Monet's worst fears seemed confirmed on noting that his sense of colour balance had changed; his pictures became dominated either by strong reds and yellows or by cooler greens and blues. Dr Coutela prescribed tinted glasses, but several pairs were rejected until, at the end of 1924, a pair made by the firm of Meyrowitz were found to be acceptable. By October 1923, Monet could discern colour to his satisfaction, and from November through to the following spring he painted feverishly. By summer, he again had difficulties in seeing certain colours. The rest of 1924 and most of 1925 were spent in deep depression, until

Right The heroic scale and intention of the Grandes Décorations provided a powerful creative stimulus in Monet's final years. A section of the great elliptical canvas *Water Lilies*: *Morning with Willows*, 1919–26, shows a radical abstraction of the water lily theme, in which the sensation of colour and light take precedence over physical form. The *plein-air* effect is enhanced by an increasingly spare application of paint, so that many of the later works seem almost to be painted on silk.

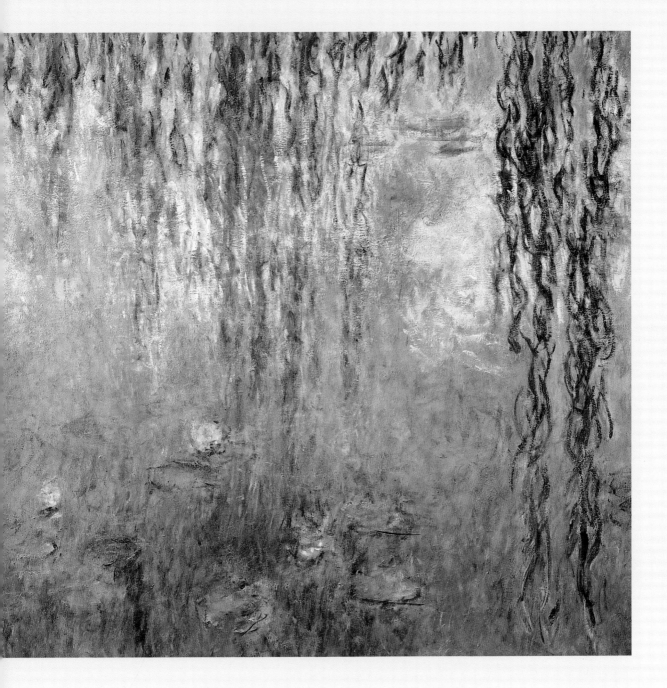

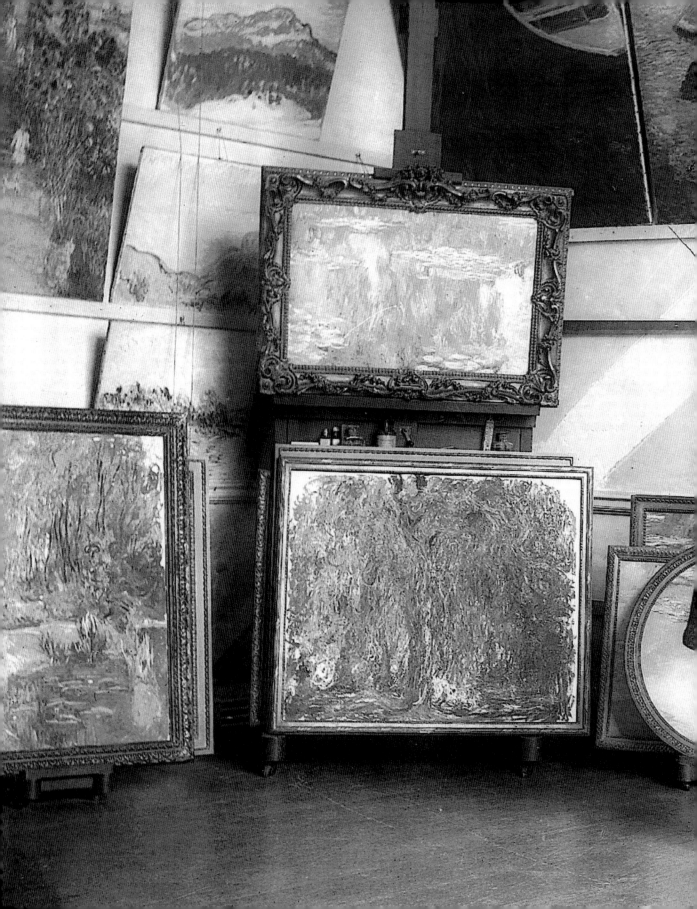

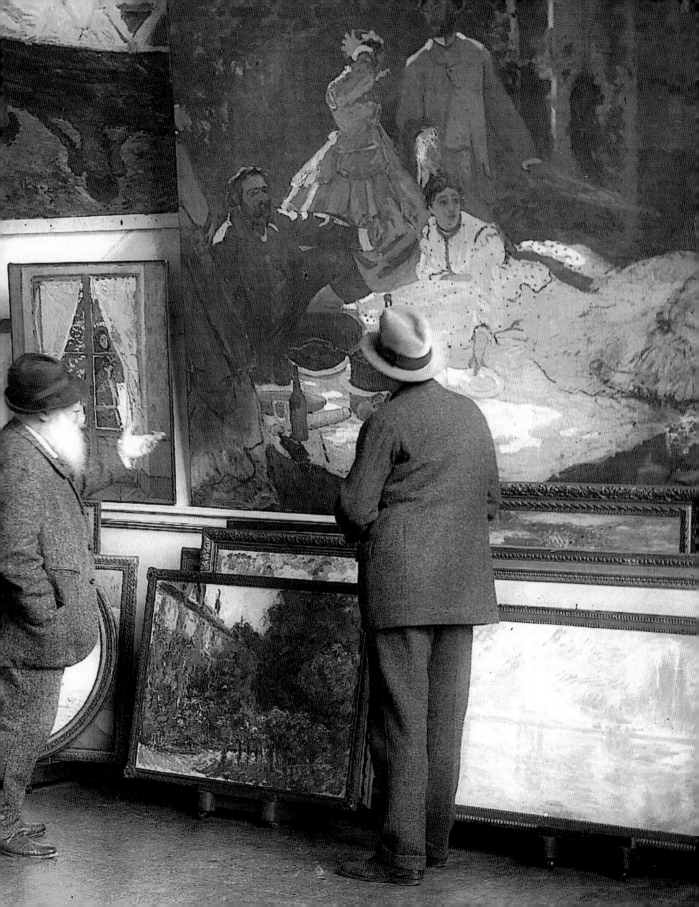

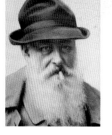

'I see blue. I no longer see red or yellow. This irritates me terribly because I know the colours exist. I know that on my palette there is some red, some yellow, a special green and a certain violet. I can no longer see them as I used to, but I recall very well the colours they gave me.'

Previous page Monet in his studio in 1920, surrounded by his paintings. The Duc de Trévise (right) examines **The Picnic on the Grass**, 1865–6; other canvases show the themes of water, flowers and foliage that dominated his later work.

Above A photograph of Monet in June 1921; the wide-brimmed hat serves to protect his eyes from the outdoor light. Despite his blunted vision, the determination in the artist's features is unmistakable.

the seeming miracle when a further pair of glasses restored his sight. These failures of physical sight may have influenced many of Monet's interviews, in which he talked of what he experienced or felt, but rarely of what he actually saw.

The *Grandes Décorations*

In the years that followed World War I, two old men rejoiced at each new season in the garden at Giverny: Clemenceau, once the radical student, who had led France to victory and armistice; and Monet, the avant-garde painter who had conserved his artistic sense of self, from the glassy surface of the pond in the 1858 *Landscape at Rouelles* to the still depths of his paintings celebrating the peace of 1918. The two panels of water lilies that were originally offered for a memorial were to reach truly vast proportions. Extending over several individ-

Right Agapanthus became naturalized along the banks of the pool at Giverny, creating an interesting contrast of texture and shape to the water lilies and willow fronds. The clear blue flowers in **Water Lilies and Agapanthus**, 1914-7, poised on their slender stems, are evocative of both water and sky.

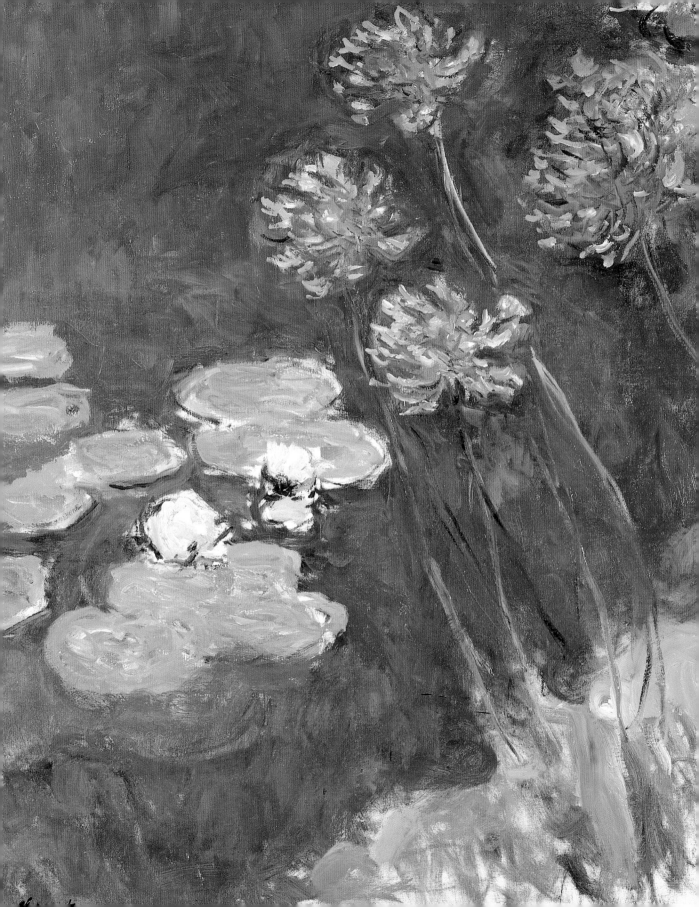

Right Monet at Giverny in 1923, recovering from his first, unsuccessful, operation to remove cataracts. Two further operations were to follow the same year which, together with tinted spectacles, significantly improved his overall vision and perception of colours. Monet was not a good patient, however, becoming frustrated and irascible for much of his recuperation.

Right Monet's deteriorating eyesight caused him severe problems in distinguishing colours for many of his final years. **The Japanese Bridge**, 1919–24, challenges the viewer with its intense, angry colours and bold use of texture. Along with the rose-alley, the bridge featured in many of Monet's last paintings at Giverny.

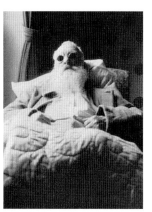

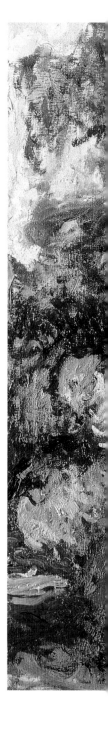

ual canvases, they would entirely cover the elliptical walls of the Orangerie's two basements in Paris. Monet had written to Clemenceau in 1918 that he was close to completion, indicating that the nation's Victory day would be an appropriate occasion for him to sign them. However, he was in fact to work on these huge encircling paintings, his *Grandes Décorations*, intensively from 1921 until his death, unaffected by the rapidly changing world beyond the walled paradise of Giverny. Confronted with such a mammoth task, he agonized and prevaricated, beseiged by artistic doubts and failing sight. But under no circumstances would Clemenceau allow him not to make this bequest to the wartorn nation. To the end he exchanged letters with Monet, as well as with the long-suffering Blanche. It was in late December 1926, just weeks after Monet's death, that the national monument of the *Grandes Décorations*, with its motif of the reflective, living waters of Giverny, was gently lifted off its stretchers in his vast studio and transferred to the walls of two galleries of the Orangerie in Paris. The formal opening took place in May 1927.

Clemenceau's commitment to the *Grandes Décorations* project was a tribute both to the bereaved nation and an esteemed friend. The Paris apartment of the former 'Tiger' of France, which now houses the Musée Clemenceau, offers a moving testimony to the men's enduring friendship. Here one can see wonderful pictures of the two men taken by the photographer Nadar, with whom Monet also maintained a long-standing friendship. There are also three paintings by Blanche Hoschedé of the flower garden and house at Giverny. Despite the museum displays, the faded décor makes the house appear

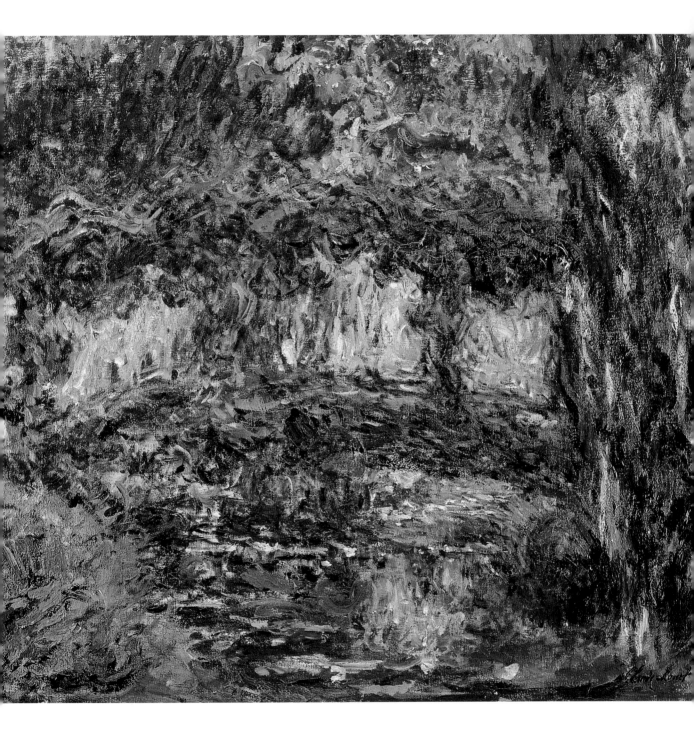

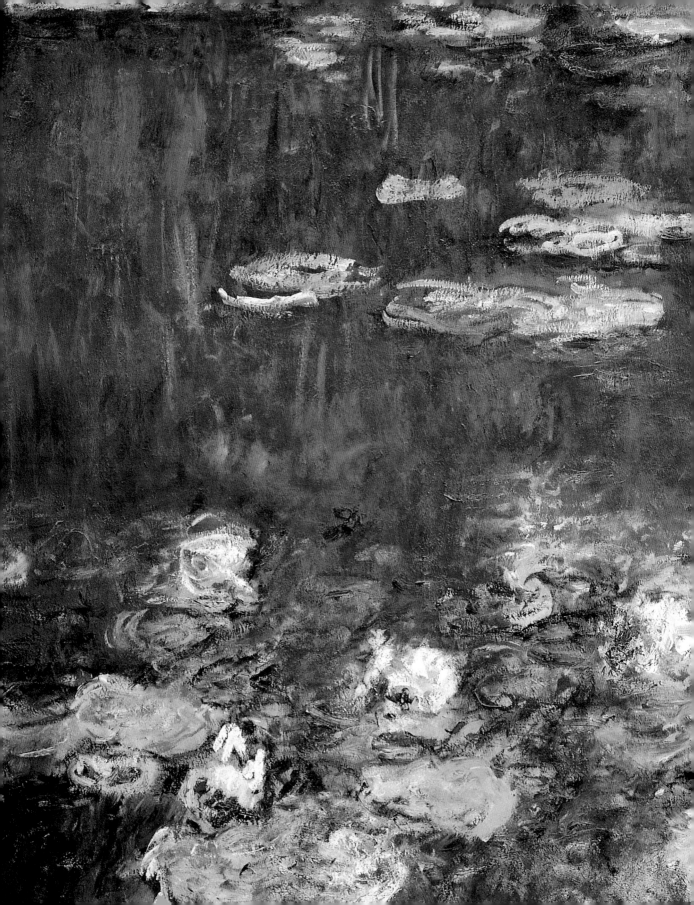